# Ninja® Foodi™ Grill
## COOKBOOK FOR BEGINNERS

# NINJA® Foodi™

## GRILL

## COOKBOOK FOR BEGINNERS

## 75 RECIPES FOR INDOOR GRILLING AND AIR FRYING PERFECTION

**Kenzie Swanhart**

Photography by Hélène Dujardin

ROCKRIDGE PRESS

Interior and Cover Designer: Joshua Moore
Art Producer: Karen Beard
Editor: Bridget Fitzgerald
Production Editor: Gleni Bartels
Photography: © 2019 Hélène Dujardin. Food styling by Tami Hardeman. Author photo courtesy of © Julien Levesque.

ISBN: Print 978-1-64152-942-6
eBook 978-1-64152-943-3

*In loving memory of Thomas Robert Ford.*

# CONTENTS

# INTRODUCTION

**THE PERFUME OF CHARCOAL LINGERS IN THE AIR AS YOU** gather with friends and family—devouring juicy, grilled burgers, charred corn slathered in butter, and all of the other eat-with-your-hands grilled goodies you expect at an all-American cookout. Later that night, as the sun begins to set and the stars line the sky like twinkle lights, you pop open a cold beverage to pair with the sizzling steaks and asparagus coming off the grill. From block parties and barbecues to warm nights full of fireflies, grilling has always been considered a summer activity. But what if it's not summer? What if the weather doesn't cooperate? What if there's no place for an outdoor grill at all?

Enter the Ninja® Foodi™ Grill, the grill that sears, sizzles, and air fry crisps.

As the head of the Culinary Innovation and Marketing team at Ninja, I am incredibly proud of the work we do to deliver five-star products that improve people's lives every day. People are at the heart of every decision we make and that leads to amazing, innovative products. Last year, we brought you the biggest innovation with the Ninja Foodi Pressure Cooker, the pressure cooker that crisps.

While the world was discovering the Foodi Pressure Cooker, we have been hard at work figuring out how we could bring that same level of innovation to indoor grilling—and let me tell you, it's good!

We at Ninja® have invented a revolutionary new way to take what you love about outdoor grilling and bring that same BTU cooking power inside—without sacrificing flavor. The Foodi™ Grill delivers a whole new way of grilling by combining super-heated cyclonic air that you know from the original Foodi, with Ninja's revolutionary high-density, ceramic-coated Grill Grate.

With the Foodi Grill, you can sear, sizzle, and air fry crisp your favorite foods with all of the flavor of outdoor grilling you love, but from the convenience of your kitchen. Plus, you get the versatility of a Ninja Foodi, so you can also Air Crisp, Bake, Roast, and Dehydrate. With the Foodi Grill, grilling is more than just dinner—now you can make Grilled Cinnamon Toast with Fresh Berries (page 38) or an Onion, Pepper, and Mushroom Frittata (page 29) for breakfast. Make snacks and appetizers like Charred Shishito Peppers (page 47), Blistered Green Beans (page 49), or Dill Pickle Chicken Wings (page 126). And let's not forget desserts, like Churros with Chocolate Sauce (page 176) and Glazed Cinnamon Biscuit Bites (page 179)—all in one talented appliance!

Are you hungry yet? You should be. I'm excited to guide you through your journey with the Foodi Grill—as a cookbook author and food blogger, but also as part of the team that invented it! I'm here to help you get started with the ultimate beginner's guide on this one-of-a-kind grilling adventure.

# 1

# Ninja® Foodi™ Grill 101

**THESE DAYS IT SEEMS THERE IS AN APPLIANCE FOR JUST** about everything, but so many machines are one-trick ponies that ultimately fail to meet our expectations. Multi-cookers have long been touted for their versatility and convenience. From slow cookers that allow you to come home to a perfectly cooked meal, to pressure cookers that cut down cook time exponentially, to the latest kitchen miracle, the air fryer. Hello fried food with less guilt— that is one train I can definitely get on (and I have)!

But what about indoor grills? Why have we accepted appliances that deliver a kitchen full of smoke and subpar food? In the past, I dismissed indoor grills because they didn't actually follow any of the principles of outdoor grilling. But the Ninja Foodi Grill is a revolutionary appliance that is changing the indoor grilling game!

This chapter will introduce you to the grill that sizzles, sears, and air fry crisps. I will break down all of the functions and benefits of the Foodi Grill so you can unleash its full potential in your kitchen— and be proud of what you cook.

# WHY THE NINJA® FOODI™ GRILL?

I have to believe that most people would grill every night if they could, but not everyone has the time for the constant back-and-forth between the grill and the kitchen, while others simply can't use an outdoor grill because of where they live.

I know firsthand how frustrating it is to try and re-create grill-like flavors indoors. Over the past 10 years, I've tried it all—pan-searing burgers that result in plumes of smoke, or using a grill pan only to be left with a greasy mess. I've tried my hand at a few indoor grills, but they consistently fall short of my expectations. It's been a struggle to cook thick cuts of meat, let alone produce the char and flavor I expect from a grill.

With the Ninja Foodi Grill, you can have your steak and eat it too—in fact, you can have sizzling steaks, sausages, char-grilled cheese-burgers, perfectly flaky fish, and even grilled corn on the cob, along with just about any other grilled favorites you can think of. And you get to enjoy them year-round, no matter the weather. It's all due to the Foodi Grill's Cyclonic Grilling Technology—and that's just one element that makes the Foodi Grill unique.

## Cyclonic Grilling Technology

What makes the Ninja Foodi Grill unlike any other indoor grill is the Cyclonic Grilling Technology, which combines a unique, high-density Grill Grate and super-heated cyclonic air that circulates rapidly around your food. This means you are searing your food to create a delicious, caramelized char, while the air cooks evenly from all sides rendering the fat and creating a crispy crust. This brings the fired-up flavors, the char-grilled greatness, and the sizzling juiciness you get from your outdoor grill—right to your kitchen.

## No-Flip Grilling

Because the Foodi Grill circulates air around your food to evenly cook all sides, in many cases, you don't even need to flip to get perfect results from top to bottom. That means, no longer having to check and guess when to flip your food. Imagine perfectly grilled fish that won't fall apart because it's cooked evenly on all sides. With No-Flip Grilling, you get perfect char marks on one side and a beautiful sear on the other. Just set your timer, walk away, and let the Foodi™ Grill cook to perfection.

## Frozen to Char-Grilled

With the Foodi Grill, you can cook your food right from the freezer. There's no need to wait around for it to thaw. Just follow the Grilling Chart (see page 189). Whether you bought flash-frozen fish at the market or pulled chicken breasts from the freezer, with the Foodi Grill you are minutes away from a delicious dinner.

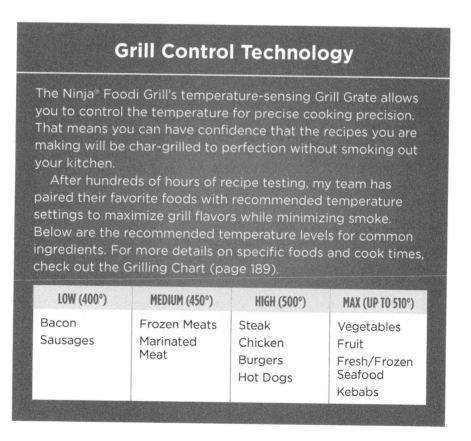

# Grill Control Technology

The Ninja® Foodi Grill's temperature-sensing Grill Grate allows you to control the temperature for precise cooking precision. That means you can have confidence that the recipes you are making will be char-grilled to perfection without smoking out your kitchen.

After hundreds of hours of recipe testing, my team has paired their favorite foods with recommended temperature settings to maximize grill flavors while minimizing smoke. Below are the recommended temperature levels for common ingredients. For more details on specific foods and cook times, check out the Grilling Chart (page 189).

| LOW (400°) | MEDIUM (450°) | HIGH (500°) | MAX (UP TO 510°) |
|---|---|---|---|
| Bacon<br>Sausages | Frozen Meats<br>Marinated<br>Meat | Steak<br>Chicken<br>Burgers<br>Hot Dogs | Vegetables<br>Fruit<br>Fresh/Frozen<br>Seafood<br>Kebabs |

### Favorites New and Old

Whether it's a perfectly grilled chicken thigh or an unexpected restaurant-inspired dish, the Foodi™ Grill's unique design makes it possible to grill just about everything, whether it's a homemade pizza or fresh fruit. You can also grill veggies directly on the Grill Grate with no special tools or accessories needed.

### Beyond Grilling

The Ninja® Foodi Grill does so much more than grill. It has the ability to Air Crisp, Bake, Roast, and Dehydrate—all in one! Air Crisp crispy, crunchy foods using little or no oil for guilt-free fried favorites. Turn your Foodi Grill into an oven to bake and roast your favorite recipes in less time. Some models can even dehydrate meats, vegetables, and fruits to make delectable homemade snacks (see page 198).

## THE NINJA FOODI GRILL

### Grill Grate

The unique Grill Grate was engineered to rapidly heat to 500°F while simultaneously circulating super-heated air. This allows you to create char marks on one side and sear all the other sides. The Ninja Foodi Grill monitors the Grill Grate's temperature to ensure even cooking while minimizing smoke. Plus, the Grill Grate is ceramic-coated for easy cleanup. Be sure to use silicone or wooden utensils so as not to scratch the Grill Grate.

### Crisper Basket

The Crisper Basket was designed so each bite comes out perfectly golden brown and crispy. Air Crisp crunchy French fries to go with your burgers or crispy Brussels sprouts to serve alongside your grilled chicken. You can also dehydrate veggie chips and jerky. Like the Grill Grate, the Crisper Basket is ceramic-coated for easy cleanup, so be sure to use silicone or wooden utensils.

**Crisper Basket**

**Grill Grate**

**Hood**

**Splatter Shield**

**Cooking Pot**

## Cooking Pot

The Foodi™ Grill's ceramic-coated Cooking Pot should always be installed when in use. When using the pot with other accessories (like the Grill Grate or Crisper Basket), be sure to clean both accessories, as oil and fat drips down into the Cooking Pot during use. As with the Grill Grate and Crisper Basket, be sure to use silicone or wooden utensils so as not to scratch the pot.

## Hood

Just like an outdoor grill, the Foodi Grill has a specially designed hood that has a convection fan that circulates air to cook ingredients from all directions. So while your food cooks directly on the hot Grill Grate, the hot air is retained and circulates. The hood also captures smoke, steam, and flavor, all of which contribute to bringing the outdoor grilling experience indoors. Plus, the hood quickly adapts with the fan and temperature, so you can Air Crisp, Bake, Roast, and Dehydrate. The powerful fan unleashes superheated air around your ingredients to crisp and caramelize them, but it can quickly adjust to slow speeds and low temperatures to dehydrate fruits, veggies, and meat for yummy sugar-free snacks.

## Splatter Shield

Located on the underside of the hood, the splatter shield keeps the heating element clean and prevents smoking. It's removable for cleaning, but always make sure it's in place when cooking.

## Grease Collector

The grease collector sits at the back of the unit to ensure that any grease trapped by the hood does not make its way to your countertop. Although you'll often find the collector completely empty, I recommend checking and cleaning it after each use.

## KNOW YOUR FUNCTIONS

Now that you're acquainted with the Ninja® Foodi™ Grill and all its parts, let's dive into the cooking functions. I outline the five different types of cooking you can do in your Foodi Grill, because it is so much more than just a grill. I also highlight how to use each function, why it is unique, and what you can look forward to making.

### Grill

At its core, the Foodi Grill is an indoor grill. To unlock unlimited grilling possibilities, use the various grill control settings. Each setting is specifically designed for different types of food. Place your Cooking Pot and Grill Grate in the Foodi Grill, then let it preheat completely before adding your food. When using the Grill function, first select the Grill Grate temperature setting:

 **Low –** Best for bacon and sausages. At your next brunch, try cooking your breakfast sides on the grill versus the skillet to keep your kitchen smoke free and your guests coming back for more.

 **Medium –** Best for frozen meats and marinated meats. I recommend Honey-Glazed Pork Tenderloin (page 154) and Bourbon Barbecue–Glazed Pork Chops (page 151).

 **High –** Best for steaks, chicken, and burgers. Run, don't walk, to my Chili-Rubbed Flank Steak (page 143), Maple-Glazed Chicken Wings (page 125), and Seared Tuna Salad (page 86).

 **Max –** Best for veggies, fruit, fresh and frozen seafood, and pizza. You're going to want to earmark the Charred Shishito Peppers (page 47), Veggie Lovers' Grilled Pizza (page 70), and Charred Peaches with Bourbon Butter Sauce (page 164).

# How to Convert Conventional Grilling Recipes

When converting your favorite grill recipes to the Ninja® Foodi™ Grill, always check the Grilling Chart (page 189), and follow the cooking temperature guidelines and recommendations. For example, use Grill High for steak, Grill Medium for marinated fresh meats, and Grill Max for fish.

Cook times should be approximately the same as what is outlined in the outdoor grill recipe, but I recommend checking your food frequently to avoid overcooking. As always, use a food thermometer to ensure that proteins are cooked to your desired level of doneness.

## Air Crisp

With Air Crisp, you can achieve that crave-worthy crispy, crunchy, golden brown texture without all the fat and oil. Use the Air Crisp feature in conjunction with the Crisper Basket to cook your favorite frozen foods—French fries, onion rings, or chicken nuggets. Air Crisp is also great for fresh vegetables, like Brussels sprouts and hand-cut French fries. Be sure to shake the Crisper Basket once or twice to ensure the crispiest, most evenly cooked results, and don't be afraid to sneak a peek under the Crisping Lid, so you can remove your food when it's crisped to your liking. New to Air Crisping? Try my Coconut Shrimp (page 105) and Crispy Chicken Cutlets (page 133).

## Bake

The Ninja Foodi Grill also works as a mini convection oven. All you need is the Cooking Pot and a cake pan to bake breads, cakes, pies, sweet treats, and more in less time than your oven. Oh, and did I mention it preheats in only 3 minutes? If you have a sweet tooth like me, dive right into dessert. I'm talking about Blueberry Cobbler (page 171). Looking for the perfect brunch potluck dish? Try my Onion, Pepper, and Mushroom Frittata (page 29).

### Roast

Use the Roast function to make everything from a slow-roasted pot roast to appetizers and even sides. Place large pieces of your protein directly in the Cooking Pot, or elevate them with the Roasting Rack accessory (page 18). Try my Southwest Stuffed Peppers (page 76).

### Dehydrate

Dehydrators can be expensive and take up a lot of space in the kitchen. With the Foodi™ Grill, you can dehydrate fruits, vegetables, meats, herbs, and more without adding another appliance to your collection.

## A GOOD GRILLING: FREQUENTLY ASKED QUESTIONS

With any new appliance comes some great questions—about the appliance, how to cook with it, and recipe hacks. These questions and answers will get you ready to use your Ninja® Foodi Grill.

### Q: How long should I preheat the Foodi Grill?

A: The Foodi Grill has a temperature-sensitive Grill Grate so that it can monitor the temperature under the hood. Always let the unit preheat completely before adding your ingredients. This takes about 8 minutes or so, depending on the temperature you have selected, and can be tracked on the preheated indicator on the control panel so you know how much time you have left. You will be prompted when the grill is completely preheated to "Add Food." Note: When the unit is warm from previously being used, it will preheat in less time.

**Q:** **If I don't have all of the ingredients for a recipe, can I swap the ingredient with something I have?**

A: I have added tips throughout the recipes in this book with ingredient swaps and suggestions. If the recipe you are making doesn't have a recipe swap noted, confirm the swap you want to make will cook in the same amount of time as the original ingredient (see the charts on pages 189). Some swaps are easier to make than others, while others may require adjusting cook times and temperatures. My advice is to experiment and have fun. After all, that's how I created these recipes!

**Q:** **How do I convert my favorite recipes to the Foodi™ Grill?**

A: You can easily convert a number of your favorite recipes to the Ninja® Foodi. Follow my recommendations on page 8 for making your favorite grill recipes in the Foodi Grill. When converting recipes from a conventional oven, use the Bake setting and reduce the temperature by 25°F. You will also likely be able to cut down the cook time. Check your food frequently to avoid overcooking.

**Q:** **Can I cook frozen food in the Foodi Grill?**

A: Yes! One of the best things about the Foodi Grill is that you can cook frozen food straight from the freezer without defrosting! Follow the charts at the back of this book for cook times for specific foods (page 189).

**Q:** **Can I Air Crisp battered ingredients?**

A: Yes, but use the proper breading technique. It is important to coat foods first with flour, then with egg, then with bread crumbs. Be sure to press the bread crumbs onto your protein so they stick in place. Loose breading may be blown off by the unit's powerful fan. Most importantly, don't forget to add some oil or cooking spray to ensure the breading gets nice and crispy!

**Q: Why is my food burned?**

A: No two pieces of protein are alike, and for that reason, they'll never cook the same. Pay close attention to the sizes of meat listed in each recipe. Proteins come in different shapes and sizes, which require different cooking times, so you may need to increase or decrease the recommended cook times to achieve desired doneness. For best results, check its progress throughout cooking, and remove food when your desired level of brownness and internal doneness (or temperature) has been achieved. Remove your food immediately after the cook time is complete to avoid overcooking.

The Ultimate Turkey Burger, *page 134*

# 2

# Get Grilling!

**YOU ARE ABOUT TO DISCOVER A WHOLE NEW WAY OF** grilling indoors. Whether you are a novice in the kitchen or a grill master, I can't wait for you to try the fired-up flavors and char-grilled greatness you will achieve with the Ninja® Foodi™ Grill.

You invited friends over for a barbecue, but the sky opened up for a summer shower? The Foodi Grill to the rescue: Grill up Jalapeño Popper Burgers (page 156), crisp up Fried Pickles (page 44) and Crispy Hand-Cut French Fries (page 59), and don't forget Rum-Soaked Grilled Pineapple Sundaes (page 162) for dessert.

Craving sizzling, juicy steaks, but it's too hot to even think about stepping out of the air-conditioning? The Foodi Grill allows you to re-create outdoor grilled flavors indoors. I recommend Filet Mignon with Pineapple Salsa (page 141) paired with the Blistered Green Beans (page 49) and a glass of chilled, dry rosé.

No outdoor space, no problem! How does Grilled Swordfish in Caper Sauce (page 98), Lemon-Garlic Artichokes (page 48), and Charred Peaches with Bourbon Butter Sauce (page 164) sound?

The Foodi Grill makes it easy to grill up breakfast, lunch, and dinner. No matter what.

# EQUIPPING YOUR KITCHEN

With the Ninja® Foodi™ Grill, you don't need a lot to create a delicious meal. By keeping a few simple ingredients and a handful of spices on hand, you can throw together a meal in minutes. Here is everything you need to get started.

## Super Simple Staples

The beauty of grilling is that the recipes use only a few simple ingredients to produce delicious, flavorful meals. I keep these staples in my fridge and pantry so that I can always cook a quick dinner or whip up a snack. Don't forget some well-marbled meats and fresh veggies.

**All-Purpose Flour –** While I keep a variety of flours on hand, if you are going to have only one, it should be all-purpose flour. Used for everything from biscuits and cookies to thickening sauces, this pantry staple lasts up to a year when stored in an airtight container.

**Barbecue Sauce –** Barbecue sauce and grilling go hand-in-hand. Keep a bottle of your favorite in the pantry or fridge. You can even create your own signature barbecue sauce, or use seasonings, fruit juice, and fruit jams to jazz up a store-bought variety.

**Bread Crumbs –** Perfect for topping casseroles and breading chicken. You can buy a prepackaged brand or save some money and make your own. Wheat, white, multigrain, or rye breads can all be turned into fresh toasted bread crumbs.

**Brown Sugar –** Brown sugar adds a subtle sweetness to a rub or sweetens up a barbecue sauce.

**Butter –** While we always have a stick or two of butter in the fridge, I also keep a few spares in the freezer—just in case. Mix butter with bread crumbs or cut butter into a pie crust, and you will be delighted not only by the flavor it brings to the dish, but also how it aids in browning and creating flaky pie crusts and biscuits that top your favorite casseroles.

**Condiments –** Condiments are not just for topping burgers. I like to use mayonnaise or mustard as a pre-rub binder, and it's a great way to inject additional moisture into your meat.

**Honey –** A common ingredient in barbecue sauce and rubs, honey can also be brushed on fruit to get the perfect caramelized crust and char-grilled result.

**Lemons –** There aren't many fresh foods on my list of pantry staples but having lemons available for fresh lemon juice is a must.

**Oil –** Just like flour, I keep a variety of oils in the pantry. When grilling, use oils with a high smoke point—canola, avocado, vegetable, or grape-seed—instead of olive oil.

## Super Simple Spice Rack

Whether you are an aspiring grill master or just looking to impress your family and friends, spice rubs are a quick and easy way to ramp up the flavor in any grilled dish. No need to invest in a bunch of specialty blends, just pick up the basics. With a few simple spices, you can create a number of seasoning blends for just about any dish.

**Basil –** Dried basil is delicious in sauces and as seasoning on chicken or other meats.

**Black Pepper –** My recipes always specify freshly ground black pepper because freshly ground peppercorns give you the fullest flavor. I have a grinder that is forever next to the stove and is constantly being refilled.

**Cayenne Pepper –** Cayenne is ground from one of the hottest varietals of dried hot peppers and is often optional in recipes. Use it sparingly to add a little spice to your dish.

**Garlic Powder –** Garlic powder is simply dehydrated garlic that is then ground. Mix with salt and you have garlic salt. Keep garlic powder in the spice rack to season a variety of veggie and chicken dishes. It is also used in a variety of spice blends.

**Ground Cinnamon –** Known for its warm, sweet flavor, cinnamon is often used in baked goods, but it also adds sweet notes to barbecue sauces and rubs.

**Ground Cumin –** Cumin is a popular aromatic spice in Middle Eastern, Asian, Mediterranean, and Mexican cuisines.

**Onion Powder –** Like garlic powder, onion powder is made from ground dehydrated onions and is used both on its own as well as in a variety of spice blends.

**Oregano –** Oregano is classified as either Mediterranean or Mexican and is often used to season dishes from these two regions.

**Paprika –** Paprika is ground from dried red bell peppers. There are different types of paprika, including smoked and sweet.

**Sea Salt –** Salt brings out the flavors in any recipe. It is used in both sweet and savory recipes throughout this book. Remember: Table salt cannot and should not be substituted 1:1 for sea salt, as it is much finer and will result in an oversalted dish.

## Super Simple Tools and Accessories

You don't need a lot to get grilling, but there are a few accessories I recommend having on hand. Below is my list of the tools and accessories for home cooks and grill masters alike.

**Basting Brush –** A basting brush is a must-have to brush and spread butter, oil, and glazes on food. If you don't have a basting brush, use a brand-new paintbrush!

**Baking Pans –** The Ninja® Foodi™ Grill is so versatile you can even bake a cake in it! And while you may not be baking a cake every night, baking pans and ramekins are handy for holding ingredients and using with other kinds of recipes, such as the Onion, Pepper, and Mushroom Frittata (page 29) or Blueberry Cobbler (page 171).

**Oven Mitts –** When things heat up, oven mitts are a must for removing accessories from the Foodi™ Grill. My favorite are mini silicone mitts because they are easy to maneuver. Remember that the Grill Grate reaches up to 500ºF, so choose a pair that is rated to that temperature.

**Meat Thermometer –** For best results, use a digital food thermometer to accurately measure the internal temperature of your protein. Insert the thermometer into the center-most and thickest part of your meat. If the meat is bone-in, insert it very close to (but not touching) the bone. Because the Foodi Grill cooks at high temperatures, proteins can overcook quickly. It's best to monitor the internal temperature of your meat, especially during the later stages of cooking.

**Skewers –** Kebab skewers are festive, fun, and a favorite on the grill. Pick up a pack of small wood skewers or opt for the stainless-steel version from Ninja® (page 18). If you opt for wood, choose the shorter size and be sure to soak them in water for at least 30 minutes before use.

**Spatula –** When it comes to flipping burgers on the grill, an angled spatula makes it all the easier. Choose a silicone option to protect the ceramic-coated Grill Grate.

**Tongs –** Whether retrieving steaks or tossing ingredients in the Crisper Basket, you will use a set of tongs every time you step up to the grill. Opt for tongs with a silicone tip.

## GET MORE OUT OF YOUR FOODI™ GRILL

In addition to the Ninja Foodi Grill accessories that came in the box, you can opt for a number of additional accessories to truly get the most out of your Foodi Grill. All of these accessories are available by going to NinjaKitchen.com.

## Griddle Plate

The Griddle Plate is the perfect companion because it transforms the Grill Grate into a flat surface. Simply place the Griddle Plate on top of the Grill Grate before preheating the Foodi™ Grill. You can make the perfect grilled cheese or a full brunch buffet complete with eggs, pancakes, and, of course, bacon. Plus, it's nonstick for easy use and cleaning.

## Veggie Tray

The Veggie Tray sits on top of the Grill Grate and is a versatile trough that can be used for just about anything. Corral peppers and onions while you grill sausages, fill it with chopped veggies and eggs for a frittata, or toss together peas and carrots with leftover rice for a quick and easy fried rice. Even better, the Grill Grate will hold up to three Veggie Trays.

## Kebab Skewers

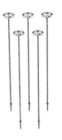

Become the ultimate grill master with these stainless-steel Kebab Skewers, which have a ring on one end to ensure that your ingredients stay secure while cooking. Pile on the veggies, chicken, steak, or lamb. I also love to make dessert skewers with fresh fruit and pound cake. Preheat the Foodi Grill, then toss the skewers onto the Grill Grate for perfectly char-grilled results.

## Roasting Rack

Place the Roasting Rack in the Cooking Pot to keep your food raised off the Grill Grate while roasting. This works great for roasting large pieces of meat and veggies. You can even slow roast a large beef roast, then finish it with high heat to get the perfect reverse sear.

### Dehydrate Rack

The Dehydrate Rack was specifically designed to expand the amount of food you can dehydrate at once. Arrange ingredients across each wire rack in a single layer, and carefully place the rack in the Cooking Pot. Follow the Dehydrating Chart (page 198) to create your own custom jerky, vegetable chips, dried fruit snacks, and more. My favorite way to use the Dehydrate Rack is to make homemade fruit leather. Simply line the wire rack with parchment paper, purée your favorite fruit, then carefully pour your fruit mixture on the lined racks.

### Multi-Purpose Pan

Perfect for baking everything from desserts to casseroles, the Multi-Purpose Pan is the must-have accessory for any Ninja® Foodi™ fanatic and can be used across most Ninja Foodi products. If you follow me on Instagram, you know the skillet cookie is my favorite recipe to make in the Multi-Purpose Pan, but you can also make cobblers, frittatas, or even a deep-dish pizza.

## THE WIDE WORLD OF INDOOR GRILLING: GETTING THE PERFECT CHAR

Before Ninja set out to redefine the indoor grilling experience, I was by no means a grilling aficionado. I could work the grill at a cookout and flip cheeseburgers, or grill steak and veggies for dinner on the patio. Throughout the development process, I learned a lot, not only about grilling, but also specifically about grilling on the Ninja® Foodi™ Grill. I learned how to achieve the perfect char and build flavor in every bite. Below I am dishing on everything I have learned so that you can be the ultimate all-season grill master.

Achieving grilling perfection with the Foodi Grill is all about getting the perfect char on your meats and veggies. I'm talking blackened meat and blistered veggies—that ideal grilled flavor that leaves you craving more.

## Don't Forget to Preheat

Like an outdoor grill, the most important step when grilling is to preheat the grill. We built a preheat indicator into the Foodi Grill so that you know when the grill is up to temperature. Be sure to keep the hood closed and let the Foodi Grill preheat until the grill tells you to "Add Food." This ensures the Grill Grate is piping hot and the air is at the optimal temperature to evenly cook your food on all sides. If you are grilling multiple rounds, allow the unit to run for 3 minutes between batches to reheat the Grill Grate.

## Oil Matters

I recommend brushing meat and veggies lightly with oil before grilling. The oil promotes charring and crisping for a perfectly sizzled and seared steak. As mentioned, for less smoke, use oils with a high smoke point—like canola, avocado, vegetable, or grape-seed—instead of olive oil. If you choose to cook ingredients at a higher temperature than recommended using olive oil, it may result in more smoke.

## Even It Out

Once you are ready to add your ingredients, evenly arrange them and space them out in a single layer to ensure consistent browning and even charring. Once you place them on the Grill Grate, gently press down to create a better sear.

## Sneak a Peek

Lift the hood while cooking to check on or flip your food. The Ninja® Foodi™ Grill will automatically pause cooking when the hood is lifted and resume when it is closed. The Foodi Grill recovers air temperature quickly, so sneak a peek often to ensure your preferred level of crispiness and doneness.

## From Frozen

There is no exact equation for grilling food from frozen, but I have included a handy section in the Grilling Chart on page 189 that outlines the prep and cook times I have found work best. When grilling frozen meats, it is best to baste them liberally and consistently with the marinade of your choosing. To get the best textures and flavors from frozen meat, season it with your favorite spice rub before grilling.

## Building Flavor

Every grill master uses their signature rub! Use spice rubs liberally. Season meat or vegetables generously, and let them sit at room temperature for 30 minutes before grilling—this will promote faster, even cooking.

## The Perfect Temp

I always advocate using a meat thermometer until you can measure doneness by lightly pressing on the meat. Keep in mind that you should always let meat rest for 5 minutes after removing it from the grill. Carry-over cooking will occur as the meat continues to cook due to residual heat. For the best results, we recommend removing your meat from the grill at about 5°F lower than your desired doneness.

| PROTEIN | COOK TO INTERNAL TEMP OF: | CARRY-OVER COOK TO INTERNAL TEMP OF: |
|---|---|---|
| Fish | 140°F | 145°F |
| Poultry | 165°F | 165°F or higher |
| Pork | 140°F | 145°F |
| Beef/Lamb (Rare) | 120°F | 125°F* |
| Beef/Lamb (Medium-Rare) | 130°F | 135°F* |
| Beef/Lamb (Medium) | 140°F | 145°F |
| Beef/Lamb (Medium-Well) | 145°F | 150°F |
| Beef/Lamb (Well) | 155°F | 160°F |
| Ground Beef | 155°F | 160°F or higher |
| Ground Pork | 155°F | 160°F |
| Ground Poultry | 165°F | 165°F or higher |

*The USDA recommends all beef be cooked to a minimum internal temperature of 145°F. If you are cooking for someone who requires meat that is cooked more thoroughly, keep this guideline in mind.

## Let It Rest

For juicy and tender results, always allow your protein to rest for 5 minutes after cooking. For roasts, half chickens, and large steaks, it's best to let them rest for 10 minutes. Resting gives the natural juices time to redistribute throughout the meat. If you carve too soon, those delicious juices end up on the cutting board instead.

## STEP BY STEP, ONE AND DONE

The Ninja® Foodi™ Grill makes it easy to create a full meal for the family, complete with a main, sides, and dessert, thanks to its ability to cook food quickly and easily using a variety of different functions. Simply grill the protein first, then set it aside to rest. While the protein rests, make a side or two to accompany the meal. Then pop dessert into the Foodi Grill and bake it to perfection while you enjoy dinner.

### Cleaning Up

To keep your Ninja Foodi Grill in tip-top shape, clean the accessories after every use. This also ensures you are ready to grill when you forget to defrost dinner and need a quick and easy meal.

The accessories that come with the Foodi Grill, including the Cooking Pot, Grill Grate, Crisper Basket, splatter shield, and cleaning brush, are dishwasher-safe, making cleanup a breeze.

If washing the accessories by hand, use the cleaning brush. The opposite end of the cleaning brush can be used as a scraper to assist with releasing baked-on sauces or cheese. Remember most of the accessories are ceramic-coated to aid in easy cleaning, so refrain from using abrasive cleaning tools. If food residue or grease are stuck on the Grill Grate, place it in the Cooking Pot and fill it with warm, soapy water. Allow it to soak for a couple hours or overnight. After soaking, use the cleaning brush to clean.

After cooking, the Foodi Grill will be hot. Leave the hood open after removing your food so it can cool while you're eating. Pro tip: After cooking, fill the pot with a pitcher of cold water to rapidly cool the unit while simultaneously soaking the Grill Grate and Cooking Pot for easy cleaning.

To clean the main unit and control panel, wipe with a damp cloth.

## ABOUT THE RECIPES

The following chapters are filled with simple, flavor-packed recipes designed to help you jump-start your Ninja® Foodi™ Grill adventure. Created to show you how to use the Foodi Grill to elevate your everyday meals, the recipes use common ingredients to create incredible meals, a number of which can be made in less than 30 minutes. You will find recipes for breakfast, snacks, and appetizers, as well as a variety of entrées and desserts. While the majority of recipes focus on the grilling feature, I have also included recipes that use the other cooking functions that make the Ninja Foodi Grill unique.

Before diving into the recipes, I want to tell you how I structured this book and how you might approach these recipes. As you begin, remember to read through each recipe completely and gather all the ingredients you need in advance. As with everything else, a little prep work before you begin to cook will save you time in the long run.

I also suggest you follow each recipe exactly as written your first time trying it. Then, as you become more comfortable with the Foodi Grill, you can switch things up and try swapping ingredients.

### Labels

I have included a variety of labels to guide you through the recipes. As appropriate, recipes are labeled Dairy-Free, Gluten-Free, Nut-Free, Vegetarian, or Vegan, so you know which recipes fit your lifestyle and which you can modify to make work for you. All recipes also include nutritional information. The recipes include the following labels as well, so you can find the perfect recipe for every meal:

**5-Ingredient** – Recipes that require five ingredients or fewer (not including salt, pepper, and oil).

**Family Favorite** – A selection of the recipes on repeat in our house.

**Under 30 Minutes** – Perfect for busy weeknights, these recipes are Foodi Grill to table in 30 minutes or less.

## Timing

The recipes that fill the following chapters include a breakdown of how long the recipe will take, start to finish. I've included the prep time and total cook time, so you can find the recipe that works best for each meal. A number of recipes use multiple cooking functions to create a full meal. Where appropriate, I have broken down the cooking time even further, so important steps are not missed.

## Accessories

I've outlined the accessories you'll use in each recipe, so you know what you need for each one. Most of these come with your Ninja® Foodi™ Grill, but you'll see I've also included a few recipes that use the Super Simple Tools and Accessories outlined on page 16.

## Tips

To help you make the most of your Foodi Grill and the recipes, I've provided my most helpful tips and tricks. You will see the following tips highlighted throughout the recipes:

**Substitution –** Follow my recommendations for swapping ingredients in and out. These are my best ideas for changing up the flavor profile or subbing ingredients for allergy reasons. Don't have honey? Try maple syrup.

**Variation –** This is where I help you customize the recipes to add a personal touch.

**Did You Know? –** Here, I showcase specific ingredients, sharing details on selecting/buying them, working with them, and storing them.

**Hack it –** My best cooking shortcuts and tricks, which will make prepping the recipe even easier.

Above all else, remember to have fun! So what are you waiting for? It's time to get grilling!

Grilled Fruit Salad with Honey-Lime Glaze, *page 28*

# Breakfast

# Grilled Fruit Salad with Honey-Lime Glaze

**SERVES 4 / PREP TIME:** 10 MINUTES / **TOTAL COOK TIME:** 4 MINUTES

*Fruit is sweet, refreshing, and delicious. Grilling makes it even better. The sugars in the fruit caramelize from the heat, intensifying their flavors. Juicy fruits can get even juicier. Serve these grilled fruits as a traditional fruit salad in a big glass bowl, layered with yogurt for the ultimate parfait, or pair it with a scoop of vanilla ice cream for dessert. Making this recipe for a party or potluck? Secure the fruit on skewers for a fun twist!*

**DAIRY-FREE, GLUTEN-FREE, NUT-FREE, VEGETARIAN, UNDER 30 MINUTES, 5-INGREDIENT**

**ACCESSORIES:** Grill Grate

**SUBSTITUTION TIP:** Just about any fruits can go on the grill as long as they are fairly firm and not overripe. Give it a try using whatever fruit you have on hand. I like using watermelon, mango, and bananas in this recipe, too.

½ pound strawberries, washed, hulled and halved

1 (9-ounce) can pineapple chunks, drained, juice reserved

2 peaches, pitted and sliced

6 tablespoons honey, divided

1 tablespoon freshly squeezed lime juice

1. Insert the Grill Grate and close the hood. Select GRILL, set the temperature to MAX, and set the time to 4 minutes. Select START/STOP to begin preheating.

2. While the unit is preheating, combine the strawberries, pineapple, and peaches in a large bowl with 3 tablespoons of honey. Toss to coat evenly.

3. When the unit beeps to signify it has preheated, place the fruit on the Grill Grate. Gently press the fruit down to maximize grill marks. Close the hood and grill for 4 minutes without flipping.

4. Meanwhile, in a small bowl, combine the remaining 3 tablespoons of honey, lime juice, and 1 tablespoon of reserved pineapple juice.

5. When cooking is complete, place the fruit in a large bowl and toss with the honey mixture. Serve immediately.

*Per serving: Calories: 178; Total fat: 1g; Saturated fat: 0g; Cholesterol: 0mg; Sodium: 3mg; Carbohydrates: 47g; Fiber: 3g; Protein: 2g*

# Onion, Pepper, and Mushroom Frittata

**SERVES 4 / PREP TIME:** 10 MINUTES / **TOTAL COOK TIME:** 10 MINUTES

*Frittatas are the ultimate clean-out-the-fridge weekend brunch or weeknight dinner recipe. Although they may sound intimidating, the truth is they are easy to make following a few simple guidelines. Not to mention, because the Ninja® Foodi™ Grill is also a mini convection oven, baking a frittata is also super quick. This classic combination of onion, pepper, and mushroom is also very versatile. Get creative and use a slice of leftover frittata as a sandwich filling, or break it up for easy breakfast tacos. You can also customize the frittata mix-ins. Try spinach, artichoke, and feta cheese, or broccoli, Cheddar, and scallion.*

**GLUTEN-FREE, NUT-FREE, VEGETARIAN, UNDER 30 MINUTES**

**ACCESSORIES:** Ninja® Multi-Purpose Pan or 8-inch baking pan

**DID YOU KNOW?**
Frittatas transport well. Whether you are meal prepping or reusing leftovers, pack them up in an airtight container and bring them for work lunches or even a picnic.

**4 large eggs**

**¼ cup whole milk**

**Sea salt**

**Freshly ground black pepper**

**½ bell pepper, seeded and diced**

**½ onion, chopped**

**4 cremini mushrooms, sliced**

**½ cup shredded Cheddar cheese**

1. In a medium bowl, whisk together the eggs and milk. Season with the salt and pepper. Add the bell pepper, onion, mushrooms, and cheese. Mix until well combined.

2. Select BAKE, set the temperature to 400°F, and set the time to 10 minutes. Select START/STOP to begin preheating.

3. Meanwhile, pour the egg mixture into the Ninja Multi-Purpose Pan or baking pan, spreading evenly.

4. When the unit beeps to signify it has preheated, place the pan directly in the pot. Close the hood and cook for 10 minutes, or until lightly golden.

*Per serving: Calories: 153; Total fat: 10g; Saturated fat: 5g; Cholesterol: 202mg; Sodium: 177mg; Carbohydrates: 5g; Fiber: 1g; Protein: 11g*

# Baked Egg and Bacon– Stuffed Peppers

**SERVES 4 / PREP TIME:** 10 MINUTES / **TOTAL COOK TIME:** 15 MINUTES

*I'm always looking for low-carb breakfast options to start the day but never have time in the morning to actually prep and cook during the week. So when I developed this recipe, I wanted to ensure that it required little prep, only 5 simple ingredients, and packed a ton of flavor. But if you are really pressed for time, you can make these stuffed peppers ahead of time and reheat them each morning.*

**GLUTEN-FREE, NUT-FREE, UNDER 30 MINUTES, 5-INGREDIENT**

**ACCESSORIES:** Crisper Basket

**DID YOU KNOW?** While all bell peppers grow from the same plant, red bell peppers are ripened the longest on the vine and green the least. Therefore, red bell peppers are the sweetest, followed by yellow and orange and, finally, green.

1 cup shredded Cheddar cheese

4 slices bacon, cooked and chopped

4 bell peppers, seeded and tops removed

4 large eggs

Sea salt

Freshly ground black pepper

Chopped fresh parsley, for garnish

1. Insert the Crisper Basket and close the hood. Select AIR CRISP, set the temperature to 390°F, and set the time to 15 minutes. Select START/STOP to begin preheating.

2. Meanwhile, divide the cheese and bacon between the bell peppers. Crack one of the eggs into each bell pepper, and season with salt and pepper.

3. When the unit beeps to signify it has preheated, place each bell pepper in the basket. Close the hood and cook for 10 to 15 minutes, until the egg whites are cooked and the yolks are slightly runny.

4. Remove the peppers from the basket, garnish with parsley, and serve.

*Per serving: Calories: 326; Total fat: 23g; Saturated fat: 10g; Cholesterol: 237mg; Sodium: 746mg; Carbohydrates: 10g; Fiber: 2g; Protein: 22g*

# Grilled Pizza with Eggs and Greens

**SERVES 2 / PREP TIME:** 10 MINUTES / **TOTAL COOK TIME:** 8 MINUTES

*Pizza for breakfast? No cold, leftover slices here. This upgraded breakfast pizza features creamy ricotta, soft-baked eggs, and fresh, peppery greens. I love the combination of textures in every bite of this dish, especially because the Ninja® Foodi™ Grill gets the crust charred, crisp, and delicious. If you prefer classic breakfast sandwich toppings, you can swap the ricotta and greens for sausage, bacon, or hash browns.*

NUT-FREE, VEGETARIAN, UNDER 30 MINUTES, FAMILY FAVORITE

**ACCESSORIES:** Grill Grate

**VARIATION TIP:** If you prefer scrambled eggs, pick up the Griddle Plate or Veggie Tray and cook the eggs first before placing them on top of the dough.

- 2 tablespoons all-purpose flour, plus more as needed
- ½ store-bought pizza dough (about 8 ounces)
- 1 tablespoon canola oil, divided
- 1 cup fresh ricotta cheese
- 4 large eggs
- Sea salt
- Freshly ground black pepper
- 4 cups arugula, torn
- 1 tablespoon extra-virgin olive oil
- 1 teaspoon freshly squeezed lemon juice
- 2 tablespoons grated Parmesan cheese

1. Insert the Grill Grate and close the hood. Select GRILL, set the temperature to MAX, and set the time to 7 minutes. Select START/STOP to begin preheating.

2. While the unit is preheating, dust a clean work surface with flour. Place the dough on the floured surface, and roll it into a 9-inch round of even thickness. Dust your rolling pin and work surface with additional flour, as needed, to ensure the dough does not stick.

3. Brush the surface of the rolled-out dough evenly with ½ tablespoon of canola oil. Flip the dough over and brush with the remaining ½ tablespoon oil. Poke the dough with a fork 5 or 6 times across its surface to prevent air pockets from forming during cooking.

CONTINUED ▶

4. When the unit beeps to signify it has preheated, place the dough on the Grill Grate. Close the hood and cook for 4 minutes.

5. After 4 minutes, flip the dough, then spoon teaspoons of ricotta cheese across the surface of the dough, leaving a 1-inch border around the edges.

6. Crack one egg into a ramekin or small bowl. This way you can easily remove any shell that may break into the egg and keep the yolk intact. Imagine the dough is split into four quadrants. Pour one egg into each. Repeat with the remaining 3 eggs. Season the pizza with salt and pepper.

7. Close the hood and continue cooking for the remaining 3 to 4 minutes, until the egg whites are firm.

8. Meanwhile, in a medium bowl, toss together the arugula, oil, and lemon juice, and season with salt and pepper.

9. Transfer the pizza to a cutting board and let it cool. Top it with the arugula mixture, drizzle with olive oil, if desired, and sprinkle with Parmesan cheese. Cut into pieces and serve.

*Per serving: Calories: 788; Total fat: 46g; Saturated fat: 16g; Cholesterol: 445mg; Sodium: 940mg; Carbohydrates: 58g; Fiber: 5g; Protein: 34g*

# Sausage Mixed Grill

**SERVES 4 / PREP TIME:** 5 MINUTES / **TOTAL COOK TIME:** 22 MINUTES

*A mixed grill is simply an assortment of grilled meats, often from a specific region or cuisine. I really love the simplicity of this recipe and how quickly it comes together. If you're looking for a high-protein, low-carb meal, this is one to try. Serve this alongside your favorite egg recipe to round out your next brunch.*

**DAIRY-FREE, GLUTEN-FREE, NUT-FREE, UNDER 30 MINUTES, 5-INGREDIENT**

**ACCESSORIES:** Grill Grate

**DID YOU KNOW?**
Sausage links are so versatile. They get their flavor from the type of meat used and the seasoning mixed into the meat when it's ground. There are many varieties available at most grocery stores. This mixed grill is a great meal any time of day. And you can make this recipe with any type of sausage that strikes your fancy. I like to poke the sausage a few times while it's cooking to ensure the casing does not burst while grilling. A knife or fork will do the trick.

8 mini bell peppers

2 heads radicchio, each cut into 6 wedges

Canola oil, for brushing

Sea salt

Freshly ground black pepper

6 breakfast sausage links

6 hot or sweet Italian sausage links

1. Insert the Grill Grate and close the hood. Select GRILL, set the temperature to MAX, and set the time to 22 minutes. Select START/STOP to begin preheating.

2. While the unit is preheating, brush the bell peppers and radicchio with the oil. Season with salt and black pepper.

3. When the unit beeps to signify it has preheated, place the bell peppers and radicchio on the Grill Grate; close the hood and cook for 10 minutes, without flipping.

4. Meanwhile, poke the sausages with a fork or knife and brush them with some of the oil.

5. After 10 minutes, remove the vegetables and set aside. Decrease the temperature to LOW. Place the sausages on the Grill Grate; close the hood and cook for 6 minutes.

6. Flip the sausages. Close the hood and cook for 6 minutes more. Remove the sausages from the Grill Grate.

7. Serve the sausages and vegetables on a large cutting board or serving tray.

*Per serving: Calories: 473; Total fat: 34g; Saturated fat: 11g; Cholesterol: 73mg; Sodium: 1051mg; Carbohydrates: 14g; Fiber: 2g; Protein: 28g*

# Sausage and Egg Loaded Breakfast Pockets

**SERVES 4 / PREP TIME:** 15 MINUTES / **TOTAL COOK TIME:** 23 MINUTES

*There's a little market in my hometown that serves the best breakfast sandwiches. Growing up, my family always stopped there to pick up the ones with bacon, egg, and cheese before a long road trip. In high school, my friends and I would sneak out for a double-double (that's double bacon, eggs, cheese, and hash browns). Even now, my cousins and I will catch up over one when I return home for a visit. These breakfast pockets combine all my favorite things about my hometown version. Easy to grab and go, they're a little reminder of home, even when I'm hundreds of miles away.*

NUT-FREE

**ACCESSORIES:** Crisper Basket

**VARIATION TIP:** Once you have the technique down, it is easy to load these breakfast pockets with your favorite breakfast sandwich toppings. Simply substitute the sausage for bacon or swap the peppers for tomato. If you want to get crazy, try adding hash browns right into the pocket.

1 (6-ounce) package ground breakfast sausage, crumbled

3 large eggs, lightly beaten

⅓ cup diced red bell pepper

⅓ cup thinly sliced scallions (green part only)

Sea salt

Freshly ground black pepper

1 (16-ounce) package pizza dough

All-purpose flour, for dusting

1 cup shredded Cheddar cheese

2 tablespoons canola oil

1. Select ROAST, set the temperature to 375ºF, and set the time to 15 minutes. Select START/STOP to begin preheating.

2. When the unit beeps to signify it has preheated, place the sausage directly in the pot. Close the hood, and cook for 10 minutes, checking the sausage every 2 to 3 minutes, breaking apart larger pieces with a wooden spoon.

**3.** After 10 minutes, pour the eggs, bell pepper, and scallions into the pot. Stir to evenly incorporate with the sausage. Close the hood and let the eggs cook for the remaining 5 minutes, stirring occasionally. Transfer the sausage and egg mixture to a medium bowl to cool slightly. Season with salt and pepper.

**4.** Insert the Crisper Basket and close the hood. Select AIR CRISP, set the temperature to 350ºF, and set the time to 8 minutes. Select START/STOP to begin preheating.

**5.** Meanwhile, divide the dough into four equal pieces. Lightly dust a clean work surface with flour. Roll each piece of dough into a 5-inch round of even thickness. Divide the sausage-egg mixture and cheese evenly among each round. Brush the outside edge of the dough with water. Fold the dough over the filling, forming a half circle. Pinch the edges of the dough together to seal in the filling. Brush both sides of each pocket with the oil.

**6.** When the unit beeps to signify it has preheated, place the breakfast pockets in the basket. Close the hood and cook for 6 to 8 minutes, or until golden brown.

*Per serving: Calories: 639; Total fat: 40g; Saturated fat: 8g; Cholesterol: 169mg; Sodium: 765mg; Carbohydrates: 50g; Fiber: 4g; Protein: 24g*

# Grilled Cinnamon Toast with Berries and Whipped Cream

**SERVES 4 / PREP TIME:** 15 MINUTES / **TOTAL COOK TIME:** 10 MINUTES

*Perhaps my favorite way to use the Ninja® Foodi™ Grill is to elevate seemingly simple recipes by bringing a whole new flavor profile to the dish. Grilling the strawberries in this recipe intensifies their flavor and caramelizes the fruit, while grilling the bread creates a smoky char that pairs perfectly with the cool, velvety whipped cream. You'll never make cinnamon toast on your stovetop again.*

DAIRY-FREE, NUT-FREE, VEGETARIAN, FAMILY FAVORITE, UNDER 30 MINUTES

ACCESSORIES: Grill Grate

SUBSTITUTION TIP:
If strawberries are not in season or you don't have them on hand, you can substitute peaches or bananas. Alternatively, skip grilling the fruit and top the cinnamon toast with blackberries, blueberries, or raspberries.

1 (15-ounce) can full-fat coconut milk, refrigerated overnight

½ tablespoon powdered sugar

1½ teaspoons vanilla extract, divided

1 cup halved strawberries

1 tablespoon maple syrup, plus more for garnish

1 tablespoon brown sugar, divided

¾ cup lite coconut milk

2 large eggs

½ teaspoon ground cinnamon

2 tablespoons unsalted butter, at room temperature

4 slices challah bread

1. Turn the chilled can of full-fat coconut milk upside down (do not shake the can), open the bottom, and pour out the liquid coconut water. Scoop the remaining solid coconut cream into a medium bowl. Using an electric hand mixer, whip the cream for 3 to 5 minutes, until soft peaks form.

2. Add the powdered sugar and ½ teaspoon of the vanilla to the coconut cream, and whip it again until creamy. Place the bowl in the refrigerator.

3. Insert the Grill Grate and close the hood. Select GRILL, set the temperature to MAX, and set the time to 15 minutes. Select START/STOP to begin preheating.

CONTINUED ▶

4. While the unit is preheating, combine the strawberries with the maple syrup and toss to coat evenly. Sprinkle evenly with ½ tablespoon of the brown sugar.

5. In a large shallow bowl, whisk together the lite coconut milk, eggs, the remaining 1 teaspoon of vanilla, and cinnamon.

6. When the unit beeps to signify it has preheated, place the strawberries on the Grill Grate. Gently press the fruit down to maximize grill marks. Close the hood and grill for 4 minutes without flipping.

7. Meanwhile, butter each slice of bread on both sides. Place one slice in the egg mixture and let it soak for 1 minute. Flip the slice over and soak it for another minute. Repeat with the remaining bread slices. Sprinkle each side of the toast with the remaining ½ tablespoon of brown sugar.

8. After 4 minutes, remove the strawberries from the grill and set aside. Decrease the temperature to HIGH. Place the bread on the Grill Grate; close the hood and cook for 4 to 6 minutes, until golden and caramelized. Check often to ensure desired doneness.

9. Place the toast on a plate and top with the strawberries and whipped coconut cream. Drizzle with maple syrup, if desired.

Per serving: *Calories: 386; Total fat: 19g; Saturated fat: 12g; Cholesterol: 97mg; Sodium: 143mg; Carbohydrates: 49g; Fiber: 2g; Protein: 7g*

# Peanut Butter Banana Chips

**MAKES 1 CUP / PREP TIME:** 10 MINUTES **/ TOTAL COOK TIME:** 8 HOURS

*The Ninja® Foodi™ Grill has earned a coveted spot on my counter, not because I like to show it off, but because it does so many things so well. While I don't use the dehydrate feature frequently, I'm always impressed when I do. It's perfect for making healthy snacks I can take with me on the go. Lately, I've been addicted to these Peanut Butter Banana Chips. They're perfect for tossing in my bag and snacking throughout the day.*

**DAIRY-FREE, GLUTEN-FREE, VEGAN, 5-INGREDIENT**

**ACCESSORIES:** Crisper Basket or Dehydrate Rack

**SUBSTITUTION TIP:** If there is an allergy or dietary preference in the house, swap the peanut butter for your nut butter of choice, or skip it all together and opt for traditional banana chips.

**2 bananas, sliced into ¼-inch rounds**

**2 tablespoons creamy peanut butter**

1. In a medium bowl, toss the banana slices with the peanut butter, until well coated. If the peanut butter is too thick and not mixing well, add 1 to 2 tablespoons of water.

2. Place the banana slices flat on the Crisper Basket or Dehydrate Rack. Arrange them in a single layer, without any slices touching each another.

3. Place the basket or rack in the pot and close the hood.

4. Select DEHYDRATE, set the temperature to 135°F, and set the time to 8 hours. Select START/STOP.

5. When cooking is complete, remove the basket or rack from the pot. Transfer the banana chips to an airtight container and store at room temperature.

*Per serving (1 cup): Calories: 398; Total fat: 17g; Saturated fat: 4g; Cholesterol: 0mg; Sodium: 149mg; Carbohydrates: 60g; Fiber: 8g; Protein: 11g*

**Fried Pickles,** *page 44*

# 4

# Snacks and Appetizers

# Fried Pickles

**SERVES 4** / **PREP TIME:** 10 MINUTES / **TOTAL COOK TIME:** 10 MINUTES

*I've been amazed by the number of things people make in an air fryer. It transports me back to our local theme park and the food stand that served up fried everything. I'm talking cookies, candy bars, pastries, and everything in between. These fried pickles are inspired by that little joint, but instead of pickle spears on a stick, this recipe uses pickle chips. On game night, serve them up with Jalapeño Popper Burgers (page 156) or alongside Dill Pickle Chicken Wings (page 126). Either way, they are sure to go fast!*

**DAIRY-FREE, NUT-FREE, VEGAN, UNDER 30 MINUTES**

**ACCESSORIES:** Crisper Basket

**HACK IT:** Serve these fried pickles with your favorite dipping sauce or dressing. Spicy ranch or creamy blue cheese works great, but you can also make your own dipping sauce by combining ¼ cup mayonnaise, 1 tablespoon horseradish, 2 teaspoons ketchup, and ¼ teaspoon Cajun seasoning.

20 dill pickle slices

¼ cup all-purpose flour

⅛ teaspoon baking powder

3 tablespoons beer or seltzer water

⅛ teaspoon sea salt

2 tablespoons water, plus more if needed

2 tablespoons cornstarch

1½ cups panko bread crumbs

1 teaspoon paprika

1 teaspoon garlic powder

¼ teaspoon cayenne pepper

2 tablespoons canola oil, divided

1. Pat the pickle slices dry, and place them on a dry plate in the freezer.

2. In a medium bowl, stir together the flour, baking powder, beer, salt, and water. The batter should be the consistency of cake batter. If it is too thick, add more water, 1 teaspoon at a time.

3. Place the cornstarch in a small shallow bowl.

4. In a separate large shallow bowl, combine the bread crumbs, paprika, garlic powder, and cayenne pepper.

**5.** Remove the pickles from the freezer. Dredge each one in cornstarch. Tap off any excess, then coat in the batter. Lastly, coat evenly with the bread crumb mixture.

**6.** Insert the Crisper Basket and close the hood. Select AIR CRISP, set the temperature to 360°F, and set the time to 10 minutes. Select START/STOP to begin preheating.

**7.** When the unit beeps to signify it has preheated, place the breaded pickles in the basket, stacking them if necessary, and gently brush them with 1 tablespoon of oil. Close the hood and cook for 5 minutes.

**8.** After 5 minutes, shake the basket and gently brush the pickles with the remaining 1 tablespoon of oil. Place the basket back in the unit and close the hood to resume cooking.

**9.** When cooking is complete, serve immediately.

**Per serving:** *Calories: 296; Total fat: 10g; Saturated fat: 1g; Cholesterol: 0mg; Sodium: 768mg; Carbohydrates: 44g; Fiber: 3g; Protein: 7g*

# Charred Shishito Peppers

**SERVES 4 / PREP TIME:** 5 MINUTES / **TOTAL COOK TIME:** 10 MINUTES

*I remember the first time I hesitantly bit into a shishito pepper and was pleasantly surprised by its bold flavor without the intense heat I expected: When my good friend Alex ordered the shishito peppers at a local tapas restaurant, I politely declined. After a bit of negotiating and peer pressure, I tried my first bite and fell in love with the blistered, salty pepper. It's now a tradition to get an order whenever they are on the menu.*

**DAIRY-FREE, GLUTEN-FREE, NUT-FREE, VEGAN, UNDER 30 MINUTES, 5-INGREDIENT**

**ACCESSORIES:** Grill Grate

**DID YOU KNOW?**
Shishito peppers are mild, until they aren't. The average shishito is about 13 to 160 times milder than a jalapeño pepper; however, about 1 out of every 10 to 20 peppers has a little extra kick.

3 cups whole shishito peppers

2 tablespoons vegetable oil

Flaky sea salt, for garnish

1. Insert the Grill Grate and close the hood. Select GRILL, set the temperature to MAX, and set the time to 10 minutes. Select START/STOP to begin preheating.

2. While the unit is preheating, in a medium bowl, toss the peppers in the oil until evenly coated.

3. When the unit beeps to signify it has preheated, place the peppers on the Grill Grate. Gently press the peppers down to maximize grill marks. Close the hood and grill for 8 to 10 minutes, until they are blistered on all sides.

4. When cooking is complete, place the peppers in a serving dish and top with the flaky sea salt. Serve immediately.

**Per serving:** *Calories: 83; Total fat: 7g; Saturated fat: 1g; Cholesterol: 0mg; Sodium: 49mg; Carbohydrates: 5g; Fiber: 3g; Protein: 2g*

# Lemon-Garlic Artichokes

**SERVES 4 / PREP TIME:** 10 MINUTES / **TOTAL COOK TIME:** 10 MINUTES

*For the longest time, I steered clear of artichokes; after all, they look more like a medieval torture device than a vegetable. But the truth is, I was too intimidated to eat them, let alone cook them. Whether you've always appreciated the artichoke's earthy flesh or you need a little motivation to give it a try, this recipe is for you. The Ninja® Foodi™ Grill grills and steams the artichoke at the same time, resulting in a tender, scrumptious treat. Serve these artichokes with aioli or your favorite dipping sauce. Enjoy every bite, as you peel off a leaf and pull away the flesh with your teeth.*

**DAIRY-FREE, GLUTEN-FREE, NUT-FREE, VEGAN, UNDER 30 MINUTES, 5-INGREDIENT**

**ACCESSORIES:** Grill Grate

**HACK IT:** With a few simple tricks, you'll be picking and prepping artichokes with ease. When shopping, choose brightly colored artichokes with tightly closed leaves. When ready to cook, snip off the thorny tips of the leaves with a pair of kitchen shears. Be sure to remove the top of the artichoke (about ¾ inch) and the stem. Pluck the bottom row of leaves, then run the artichoke under cold water to rinse. Voilà, you are ready to get grilling!

Juice of ½ lemon

½ cup canola oil

3 garlic cloves, chopped

Sea salt

Freshly ground black pepper

2 large artichokes, trimmed and halved

1. Insert the Grill Grate and close the hood. Select GRILL, set the temperature to MAX, and set the time to 10 minutes. Select START/STOP to begin preheating.

2. While the unit is preheating, in a medium bowl, combine the lemon juice, oil, and garlic. Season with salt and pepper, then brush the artichoke halves with the lemon-garlic mixture.

3. When the unit beeps to signify it has preheated, place the artichokes on the Grill Grate, cut side down. Gently press them down to maximize grill marks. Close the hood and grill for 8 to 10 minutes, occasionally basting generously with the lemon-garlic mixture throughout cooking, until blistered on all sides.

*Per serving: Calories: 285; Total fat: 28g; Saturated fat: 2g; Cholesterol: 0mg; Sodium: 137mg; Carbohydrates: 10g; Fiber: 5g; Protein: 3g*

# Blistered Green Beans

**SERVES 4 / PREP TIME:** 5 MINUTES / **TOTAL COOK TIME:** 10 MINUTES

*Things are better with a little bit of char. That is why I prefer a roasted marshmallow or toasted bread to the alternative. The same is true with vegetables, which is why my favorite way to enjoy my greens is off the grill or out of the oven. Grilling intensifies the flavor of vegetables and kisses them with a little smoky char. No need for fancy marinades or dipping sauces here—let the vegetables take center stage.*

DAIRY-FREE, GLUTEN-FREE, NUT-FREE, VEGAN, UNDER 30 MINUTES, 5-INGREDIENT

ACCESSORIES: Grill Grate

DID YOU KNOW? With most grills, you would need a grilling basket to contain the green beans, so they don't fall into the flame, but the Ninja® Foodi™ Grill Grate was specifically designed so that you can grill small vegetables without extra accessories.

1 pound *haricots verts* or green beans, trimmed

2 tablespoons vegetable oil

Juice of 1 lemon

Pinch red pepper flakes

Flaky sea salt

Freshly ground black pepper

1. Insert the Grill Grate and close the hood. Select GRILL, set the temperature to MAX, and set the time to 10 minutes. Select START/STOP to begin preheating.

2. While the unit is preheating, in a medium bowl, toss the green beans in oil until evenly coated.

3. When the unit beeps to signify it has preheated, place the green beans on the Grill Grate. Close the hood and grill for 8 to 10 minutes, tossing frequently until blistered on all sides.

4. When cooking is complete, place the green beans on a large serving platter. Squeeze lemon juice over the green beans, top with red pepper flakes, and season with sea salt and black pepper.

*Per serving: Calories: 100; Total fat: 7g; Saturated Fat: 1g; Cholesterol: 0mg; Sodium: 30mg; Carbohydrates: 10g; Fiber: 4g; Protein: 2g*

# Bacon Brussels Sprouts

**SERVES 4 / PREP TIME:** 10 MINUTES / **TOTAL COOK TIME:** 12 MINUTES

*This is one of the first recipes I mastered years ago. In fact, a version of it made an appearance in my very first cookbook,* Paleo in 28, *and it remains a reader favorite and a favorite in our house. I updated the recipe here to work with your Ninja® Foodi™ Grill. You will love the way the Brussels sprouts crisp up, while the bacon renders and fills the nooks and crannies of every bite with delicious bacon-y goodness.*

DAIRY-FREE, GLUTEN-FREE, NUT-FREE, UNDER 30 MINUTES, FAMILY FAVORITE, 5-INGREDIENT

**ACCESSORIES:** Crisper Basket

**HACK IT:** During the week, dirty dishes are my nemesis. I have a simple trick to avoid using dishes all together in this recipe. In step 2, place the ingredients in a plastic bag instead of a bowl. Shake to coat, then pour them directly into the Crisper Basket—*voilà!*

1 pound Brussels sprouts, trimmed and halved

2 tablespoons extra-virgin olive oil

1 teaspoon sea salt

½ teaspoon freshly ground black pepper

6 slices bacon, chopped

1. Insert the Crisper Basket and close the hood. Select AIR CRISP, set the temperature to 390ºF, and set the time to 12 minutes. Select START/STOP to begin preheating.

2. Meanwhile, in a large bowl, toss the Brussels sprouts with the olive oil, salt, pepper, and bacon.

3. When the unit beeps to signify it has preheated, add the Brussels sprouts to the basket. Close the hood and cook for 10 minutes.

4. After 6 minutes, shake the basket of Brussels sprouts. Place the basket back in the unit and close the hood to resume cooking.

5. After 6 minutes, check for desired crispness. Continue cooking up to 2 more minutes, if necessary.

*Per serving: Calories: 264; Total fat: 19g; Saturated fat: 5g; Cholesterol: 31mg; Sodium: 1155mg; Carbohydrates: 11g; Fiber: 4g; Protein: 15g*

# Grilled Asian-Style Broccoli

**SERVES 4 / PREP TIME:** 10 MINUTES / **TOTAL COOK TIME:** 10 MINUTES

*Grilling is often associated with hamburgers, hot dogs, and all of the various meats that we enjoy charred and crisped to perfection. But what about the vegetables? This Grilled Asian-Style Broccoli is the perfect complement to any grilled meal. It's sweet and salty smokiness will sure get your taste buds dancing. I love to pair this recipe with Chili-Rubbed Flank Steak (page 143) or Charred Korean-Style Steak Tips (page 155).*

DAIRY-FREE, NUT-FREE, VEGAN, UNDER 30 MINUTES, FAMILY FAVORITE

ACCESSORIES: Grill Grate

VARIATION TIP: There are so many ways to put your own twist on this recipe and many of the grilled recipes throughout this book. Switch up the seasoning or swap out the broccoli all together (try cauliflower or Brussels sprouts). Remember that when you are making substitutions, you may need to adjust the cooking times. Check the Grilling Charts (page 189) and keep an eye on what you're cooking, so that it's crisped and charred to your liking.

4 tablespoons soy sauce

4 tablespoons balsamic vinegar

2 tablespoons canola oil

2 teaspoons maple syrup

2 heads broccoli, trimmed into florets

Red pepper flakes, for garnish

Sesame seeds, for garnish

1. Insert the Grill Grate and close the hood. Select GRILL, set the temperature to MAX, and set the time to 10 minutes. Select START/STOP to begin preheating.

2. While the unit is preheating, in a large bowl, whisk together the soy sauce, balsamic vinegar, oil, and maple syrup. Add the broccoli and toss to coat evenly.

3. When the unit beeps to signify it has preheated, place the broccoli on the Grill Grate. Close the hood and grill for 8 to 10 minutes, until charred on all sides.

4. When cooking is complete, place the broccoli on a large serving platter. Garnish with red pepper flakes and sesame seeds. Serve immediately.

*Per serving: Calories: 133; Total fat: 8g; Saturated fat: 1g; Cholesterol: 0mg; Sodium: 948mg; Carbohydrates: 13g; Fiber: 4g; Protein: 5g*

# Honey-Glazed Grilled Carrots

**SERVES 4 / PREP TIME:** 10 MINUTES / **TOTAL COOK TIME:** 10 MINUTES

*I'm usually not a fan of carrots unless they make an appearance inside a warm cake topped with cream cheese frosting. It's difficult to get texture on carrots, while ensuring they are cooked through. Gone are the days of hiding vegetables in napkins and feeding them to the dog. These carrots are roasted in a sticky sweet glaze and charred to perfection. At your next holiday, wow your family with Honey-Glazed Grilled Carrots instead of the traditional steamed variety.*

GLUTEN-FREE, NUT-FREE, VEGETARIAN, UNDER 30 MINUTES, 5-INGREDIENT

**ACCESSORIES:** Grill Grate

**SUBSTITUTION TIP:**
You can easily modify the glaze in this recipe to fit with your dietary preferences, like omitting the butter and brown sugar, or you can skip the glaze all together and add fresh herbs instead.

**6 medium carrots, peeled and cut lengthwise**

**1 tablespoon canola oil**

**2 tablespoons unsalted butter, melted**

**¼ cup brown sugar, melted**

**¼ cup honey**

**⅛ teaspoon sea salt**

1. Insert the Grill Grate and close the hood. Select GRILL, set the temperature to MAX, and set the time to 10 minutes. Select START/STOP to begin preheating.

2. In a large bowl, toss the carrots and oil until well coated.

3. When the unit beeps to signify it has preheated, place carrots on the center of the Grill Grate. Close the hood and cook for 5 minutes.

4. Meanwhile, in a small bowl, whisk together the butter, brown sugar, honey, and salt.

5. After 5 minutes, open the hood and baste the carrots with the glaze. Using tongs, turn the carrots and baste the other side. Close the hood and cook for another 5 minutes.

6. When cooking is complete, serve immediately.

*Per serving: Calories: 218; Total fat: 9g; Saturated fat: 4g; Cholesterol: 15mg; Sodium: 119mg; Carbohydrates: 35g; Fiber: 2g; Protein: 1g*

# Garlicky Summer Squash and Charred Red Onion

**SERVES 4 / PREP TIME:** 15 MINUTES / **TOTAL COOK TIME:** 15 MINUTES

*Grilled squash and onions are a simple, tasty addition to any menu. The combination of hearty squash and sweet charred onion go great alongside most grilled meats, adding a pop of color and flavor. Or, make these as elevated toppings for your next burger bar! The squash and onion hold up on the Ninja® Foodi™ Grill and can be served hot or cold—there are no rules here!*

GLUTEN-FREE, NUT-FREE, VEGETARIAN, UNDER 30 MINUTES

ACCESSORIES: Grill Grate

SUBSTITUTION TIP: If summer squash is out of season or just doesn't look appealing at the market, swap it out for zucchini, which is much more widely available.

- ½ cup vegetable oil, plus 3 tablespoons
- ¼ cup white wine vinegar
- 1 garlic clove, grated
- 2 summer squash, sliced lengthwise about ¼-inch thick
- 1 red onion, peeled and cut into wedges
- Sea salt
- Freshly ground black pepper
- 1 (8-ounce) package crumbled feta cheese
- Red pepper flakes

1. Insert the Grill Grate and close the hood. Select GRILL, set the temperature to MAX, and set the time to 15 minutes. Select START/STOP to begin preheating.

2. Meanwhile, in a small bowl, whisk together ½ cup oil, vinegar, and garlic, and set aside.

3. In a large bowl, toss the squash and onion with remaining 3 tablespoons of oil until evenly coated. Season with the salt and pepper.

4. When the unit beeps to signify it has preheated, arrange the squash and onions on the Grill Grate. Close the hood and cook for 6 minutes.

**5.** After 6 minutes, open the hood and flip the squash. Close the hood and cook for 6 to 9 minutes more.

**6.** When vegetables are cooked to desired doneness, remove them from the grill. Arrange the vegetables on a large platter and top with the feta cheese. Drizzle the dressing over the top, and sprinkle with the red pepper flakes. Let stand for 15 minutes before serving.

*Per serving: Calories: 521; Total fat: 50g; Saturated fat: 16g; Cholesterol: 50mg; Sodium: 696mg; Carbohydrates: 11g; Fiber: 2g; Protein: 10g*

# Crispy Rosemary Potatoes

**SERVES 4 / PREP TIME:** 10 MINUTES / **TOTAL COOK TIME:** 20 MINUTES

*The best recipes are not beholden to a specific meal or time of day. I'm talking about the homemade pancake recipe you bust out at dinner or the diner cheeseburger you order for breakfast. These Crispy Rosemary Potatoes are the perfect side to any meal, any time of day—including as a snack! Packed with flavor, I love pairing these crispy little bites with Baked Egg and Bacon–Stuffed Peppers (page 31) or Bourbon Barbecue–Glazed Pork Chops (page 151).*

---

DAIRY-FREE, GLUTEN-FREE, NUT-FREE, VEGAN, FAMILY FAVORITE, UNDER 30 MINUTES

---

**ACCESSORIES:** Crisper Basket

---

**HACK IT:** Pre-made spice blends are the ultimate time-saver and prep hack. If you are looking to save time, skip the spices listed in this recipe and opt for a packaged onion soup mix instead. Just add 1 teaspoon dried rosemary, and you are good to go!

**2 pounds baby red potatoes, quartered**

**2 tablespoons extra-virgin olive oil**

**¼ cup dried onion flakes**

**1 teaspoon dried rosemary**

**½ teaspoon onion powder**

**½ teaspoon garlic powder**

**¼ teaspoon celery celery**

**¼ teaspoon freshly ground black pepper**

**½ teaspoon dried parsley**

**½ teaspoon sea salt**

1. Insert the Crisper Basket and close the hood. Select AIR CRISP, set the temperature to 390ºF, and set the time to 20 minutes. Select START/STOP to begin preheating.

2. Meanwhile, place all the ingredients in a large bowl and toss until evenly coated.

3. When the unit beeps to signify it has preheated, add the potatoes to the basket. Close the hood and cook for 10 minutes.

4. After 10 minutes, shake the basket well. Place the basket back in the unit and close the hood to resume cooking.

5. After 10 minutes, check for desired crispness. Continue cooking up to 5 minutes more, if necessary.

---

*Per serving: Calories: 232; Total fat: 7g; Saturated fat: 1g; Cholesterol: 0mg; Sodium: 249mg; Carbohydrates: 39g; Fiber: 6g; Protein: 4g*

# Grilled Heirloom Tomato BLT

**SERVES 4 / PREP TIME:** 10 MINUTES / **TOTAL COOK TIME:** 10 MINUTES

*In this BLT, the bread is grilled, adding an extra layer of flavor. We also grill the tomatoes, adding yet more texture and smoky flavor throughout every bite. Layered with crisp fresh lettuce, creamy mayo, and salty bacon, the BLT will always be a classic.*

DAIRY-FREE, NUT-FREE, UNDER 30 MINUTES

ACCESSORIES: Grill Grate

VARIATION TIP: Add a squeeze of lemon juice and a hint of lemon zest to the mayo for a little brightness.

8 slices white bread

8 tablespoons mayonnaise

2 heirloom tomatoes, sliced ¼-inch thick

2 tablespoons canola oil

Sea salt

Freshly ground black pepper

8 slices bacon, cooked

8 leaves iceberg lettuce

1. Insert the Grill Grate, and close the hood. Select GRILL, set the temperature to MAX, and set the time to 10 minutes. Select START/STOP to begin preheating.

2. While the unit is preheating, spread a thin layer of mayonnaise on one side of each piece of bread.

3. When the unit beeps to signify it has preheated, place the bread, mayonnaise-side down, on the Grill Grate. Close the hood and cook for 2 to 3 minutes, until crisp.

4. Meanwhile, remove the watery pulp and seeds from the tomato slices. Brush both sides of the tomatoes with the oil and season with salt and pepper.

5. After 2 to 3 minutes, remove the bread and place the tomatoes on the grill. Close the hood and continue cooking for the remaining 6 to 8 minutes.

6. To assemble, spread a thin layer of mayonnaise on the non-grilled sides of the bread. Layer the tomatoes, bacon, and lettuce on the bread, and top with the remaining slices of bread. Slice each sandwich in half and serve.

*Per serving: Calories: 625; Total fat: 45g; Saturated fat: 9g; Cholesterol: 52mg; Sodium: 1483mg; Carbohydrates: 35g; Fiber: 3g; Protein: 20g*

# Crispy Hand-Cut French Fries

**SERVES 4 / PREP TIME:** 15 MINUTES, PLUS 30 MINUTES TO SOAK
**TOTAL COOK TIME:** 25 MINUTES

*Is there anything more delightful than perfectly crisp French fries—crunchy on the outside and fluffy on the inside? The Air Crisp feature on the Ninja® Foodi™ Grill is my go-to for reheating leftover fries, grabbing a bag from the freezer, or slicing potatoes for a homemade version. Try your hand at this recipe, then put your own twist on it by swapping out the russet potatoes for sweet potatoes, parsnip, or yuca. Pair your root veggie fries with any of the entrées in this book.*

DAIRY-FREE, GLUTEN-FREE, NUT-FREE, VEGAN, 5-INGREDIENT

**ACCESSORIES:** Crisper Basket

**HACK IT:** If you don't have a French fry press at home, you can quickly cut French fries by first using an apple slicer. This will break the potatoes down to a workable size. Or just stick with the apple slicer and make steak fries—increase the cook time if you increase the size of the fry.

**1 pound russet or Idaho potatoes, cut in 2-inch strips**

**3 tablespoons canola oil**

1. Place the potatoes in a large bowl and cover them with cold water. Let soak for 30 minutes. Drain well, then pat with a paper towel until very dry.

2. Insert the Crisper Basket and close the hood. Select AIR CRISP, set the temperature to 390°F, and set the time to 25 minutes. Select START/STOP to begin preheating.

3. Meanwhile, in a large bowl, toss the potatoes with the oil.

4. When the unit beeps to signify it has preheated, add the potatoes to the basket. Close the hood and cook for 10 minutes.

5. After 10 minutes, shake the basket well. Place the basket back in the unit and close the hood to resume cooking.

6. After 10 minutes, check for desired crispness. Continue cooking up to 5 minutes more, if necessary.

7. When cooking is complete, serve immediately with your favorite dipping sauce.

*Per serving: Calories: 171; Total fat: 11g; Saturated fat: 1g; Cholesterol: 0mg; Sodium: 7mg; Carbohydrates: 18g; Fiber: 3g; Protein: 2g*

# Sweet Potato Chips

**MAKES 1 CUP / PREP TIME:** 10 MINUTES / **TOTAL COOK TIME:** 8 TO 10 HOURS

*I developed this recipe for one reason, and it's a good one—my mom asked me to. The moment she found out we were working on a product with a dehydrate feature, she asked me for the best sweet potato chip recipe. Like the good daughter I am, I started working on a recipe. The beauty of this recipe is its simplicity and the ability to customize it by simply adding your favorite spices.*

**DAIRY-FREE, GLUTEN-FREE, NUT-FREE, VEGAN, 5-INGREDIENT**

**ACCESSORIES:** Crisper Basket or Dehydrating Rack

**VARIATION TIP:** Walking down the chip aisle, it seems there is a different flavor for just about everyone. Re-create your favorite flavors by adding cinnamon, onion powder, smoked paprika, or any combination of seasonings of your choice in step 2.

1 sweet potato, peeled

½ tablespoon avocado oil

½ teaspoon sea salt

1. Using a mandoline, thinly slice (⅛ inch or less) the sweet potato.

2. In a large bowl, toss the sweet potato slices with the oil until evenly coated. Season with the salt.

3. Place the sweet potato slices flat on the Crisper Basket or dehydrating rack. Arrange them in a single layer, without any slices touching each other.

4. Place the basket or rack in the pot and close the hood.

5. Select DEHYDRATE, set the temperature to 120°F, and set the time to 10 hours. Select START/STOP.

6. After 8 hours, check for desired doneness. Continue dehydrating for 2 more hours, if necessary.

7. When cooking is complete, remove the basket or rack from the pot. Transfer the sweet potato chips to an airtight container and store at room temperature.

*Per serving (1 cup): Calories: 174; Total fat: 7g; Saturated fat: 1g; Cholesterol: 0mg; Sodium: 1008mg; Carbohydrates: 26g; Fiber: 4g; Protein: 2g*

Veggie Lovers' Grilled Pizza, *page 70*

# 5

# Vegetarian

# Loaded Potato and Grilled Corn Chowder

**SERVES 4 / PREP TIME:** 15 MINUTES / **TOTAL COOK TIME:** 50 MINUTES

*When corn is at its peak, the only way to elevate it further is to put it on the grill. Grilled corn in the Ninja® Foodi™ Grill is perfectly sweet, with a hint of smoky char. Here, I've transformed this barbecue staple into a creamy, delicious, and hearty soup. For the fully loaded potato soup experience, top it off with shredded Cheddar cheese and, if you're not following a vegetarian diet, crispy, crumbled bacon.*

**GLUTEN-FREE, NUT-FREE, VEGETARIAN**

**ACCESSORIES:** Grill Grate, Crisper Basket

**HACK IT:** Removing the kernels from a corn cob is straightforward. Hold a corn cob vertically and use a sharp knife to cut from top to bottom. Rotate the cob until all the kernels are removed. Another trick is to place the ear of corn in the center opening of a tube or Bundt pan. Cut downward so the kernels fall into the pan while the cob is firmly secured.

**4 ears corn, shucked**

**2 tablespoons canola oil**

**1½ teaspoons sea salt, plus additional to season the corn**

**½ teaspoon freshly ground black pepper, plus additional to season the corn**

**3 tablespoons unsalted butter**

**1 small onion, finely chopped**

**2½ cups vegetable broth**

**1½ cups milk**

**4 cups diced potatoes**

**2 cups half-and-half**

**1½ teaspoons chopped fresh thyme**

**1.** Insert the Grill Grate and close the hood. Select GRILL, set the temperature to MAX, and set the time to 12 minutes. Select START/STOP to begin preheating.

**2.** While the unit is preheating, brush each ear of corn with ½ tablespoon of oil. Season the corn with salt and pepper to taste.

**3.** When the unit beeps to signify it has preheated, place the corn on the Grill Grate and close the hood. Cook for 6 minutes.

**4.** After 6 minutes, flip the corn. Close the hood and continue cooking for the remaining 6 minutes.

**5.** When cooking is complete, remove the corn and let cool. Cut the kernels from the cobs.

**6.** In a food processor, purée 1 cup of corn kernels until smooth.

**7.** In a large pot over medium-high heat, melt the butter. Add the onion and sauté until soft, 5 to 7 minutes. Add the broth, milk, and potatoes. Bring to a simmer and cook until the potatoes are just tender, 10 to 12 minutes. Stir in the salt and pepper.

**8.** Stir in the puréed corn, remaining corn kernels, and half-and-half. Bring to a simmer and cook, stirring occasionally, until the potatoes are cooked through, 15 to 20 minutes.

**9.** Using a potato masher or immersion blender, slightly mash some of the potatoes. Stir in the thyme, and additional salt and pepper to taste.

**Per serving:** *Calories: 586; Total fat: 33g; Saturated fat: 16g; Cholesterol: 75mg; Sodium: 692mg; Carbohydrates: 64g; Fiber: 9g; Protein: 14g*

# Cheesy Ranch Cauliflower Steaks

**SERVES 2 / PREP TIME:** 10 MINUTES / **TOTAL COOK TIME:** 15 MINUTES

*Cauliflower is having a moment right now, whether transformed into cauliflower tots, cauliflower rice, or cauliflower steaks. When you grill cauliflower steaks, the intense heat softens and caramelizes the vegetable from stem to floret until it becomes tender and almost sweet. Because cauliflower steaks are held together by the piece of stem at the base of each head, you can only cut two thick steaks per cauliflower. If you want to serve four, simply double the recipe.*

**GLUTEN-FREE, NUT-FREE, UNDER 30 MINUTES**

**ACCESSORIES:** Grill Grate

**HACK IT:** For a shockingly delicious vegetable snack, toss any extra cauliflower florets in the oil mixture, then grill, turning occasionally, for about 6 minutes, until charred and tender.

1 head cauliflower, stemmed and leaves removed

¼ cup canola oil

½ teaspoon garlic powder

½ teaspoon paprika

Sea salt

Freshly ground black pepper

1 cup shredded Cheddar cheese

Ranch dressing, for garnish

4 slices bacon, cooked and crumbled

2 tablespoons chopped fresh chives

1. Cut the cauliflower from top to bottom into two 2-inch "steaks"; reserve the remaining cauliflower to cook separately.

2. Insert the Grill Grate and close the hood. Select GRILL, set the temperature to MAX, and set the time to 15 minutes. Select START/STOP to begin preheating.

3. Meanwhile, in a small bowl, whisk together the oil, garlic powder, and paprika. Season with salt and pepper. Brush each steak with the oil mixture on both sides.

**4.** When the unit beeps to signify it has preheated, place the steaks on the Grill Grate. Close the hood and cook for 10 minutes.

**5.** After 10 minutes, flip the steaks and top each with ½ cup of cheese. Close the hood and continue to cook until the cheese is melted, about 5 minutes.

**6.** When cooking is complete, place the cauliflower steaks on a plate and drizzle with the ranch dressing. Top with the bacon and chives.

**Per serving:** *Calories: 721; Total fat: 62g; Saturated fat: 19g; Cholesterol: 101mg; Sodium: 1555mg; Carbohydrates: 11g; Fiber: 4g; Protein: 32g*

# Grilled Eggplant, Tomato, and Mozzarella Stacks

**SERVES 4 / PREP TIME:** 10 MINUTES **/ TOTAL COOK TIME:** 14 MINUTES

*A twist on a classic eggplant Parmesan, this recipe is as simple as it is delicious. The smoky char from the grill pairs well with the creamy buffalo mozzarella, while the acidic tomatoes add brightness to each bite. A sprinkle of basil and sea salt finishes things off.*

GLUTEN-FREE, NUT-FREE, VEGETARIAN, UNDER 30 MINUTES, 5-INGREDIENT

ACCESSORIES: Grill Grate

1 eggplant, sliced ¼-inch thick

2 tablespoons canola oil

2 beefsteak or heirloom tomatoes, sliced ¼-inch thick

12 large basil leaves

½ pound buffalo mozzarella, sliced ¼-inch thick

Sea salt

1. Insert the Grill Grate and close the hood. Select GRILL, set the temperature to MAX, and set the time to 14 minutes. Select START/STOP to begin preheating.

2. Meanwhile, in a large bowl, toss the eggplant and oil until evenly coated.

3. When the unit beeps to signify it has preheated, place the eggplant on the Grill Grate. Close the hood and grill for 8 to 12 minutes, until charred on all sides.

4. After 8 to 12 minutes, top the eggplant with one slice each of tomato and mozzarella. Close the hood and grill for 2 minutes, until the cheese melts.

5. When cooking is complete, remove the eggplant stacks from the grill. Place 2 or 3 basil leaves on top of half of the stacks. Place the remaining eggplant stacks on top of those with basil so that there are four stacks total. Season with salt, garnish with the remaining basil, and serve.

*Per serving: Calories: 284; Total Fat: 20g; Saturated Fat: 8g; Cholesterol: 45mg; Sodium: 420mg; Carbohydrates: 13g; Fiber: 6g; Protein: 15g*

# Veggie Lovers' Grilled Pizza

**SERVES 2 / PREP TIME:** 10 MINUTES / **TOTAL COOK TIME:** 10 MINUTES

*Looking for an easy way to sneak a few more veggies into the day? How about on top of a super-quick pizza? I love this recipe because it starts with store-bought pizza dough, so you're halfway to dinner already. It's also a great way to use the veggies still in the refrigerator at the end of the week. Because the dough cooks so quickly, you can make a number of these pizzas back to back. Set up a topping bar and let everyone in the family customize their pizza with their favorite toppings.*

NUT-FREE, VEGETARIAN, UNDER 30 MINUTES

ACCESSORIES: Grill Grate

HACK IT: Many grocery stores sell both fresh and frozen dough, but if you can't find it, ask your local pizza joint to sell you some. For best results, remember to bring the dough to room temperature before rolling it out. This makes it easier to work with and keeps it from shrinking back during the stretching process.

2 tablespoons all-purpose flour, plus more as needed

½ store-bought pizza dough (about 8 ounces)

1 tablespoon canola oil, divided

½ cup pizza sauce

1 cup shredded mozzarella cheese

½ zucchini, thinly sliced

½ red onion, sliced

½ red bell pepper, seeded and thinly sliced

1. Insert the Grill Grate and close the hood. Select GRILL, set the temperature to MAX, and set the time to 7 minutes. Select START/STOP to begin preheating.

2. While the unit is preheating, dust a clean work surface with the flour.

3. Place the dough on the floured surface, and roll it into a 9-inch round of even thickness. Dust your rolling pin and work surface with additional flour, as needed, to ensure the dough does not stick.

4. Evenly brush the surface of the rolled-out dough with ½ tablespoon of oil. Flip the dough over and brush the other side with the remaining ½ tablespoon of oil. Poke the dough with a fork 5 or 6 times across its surface to prevent air pockets from forming while it cooks.

5. When the unit beeps to signify it has preheated, place the dough on the Grill Grate. Close the hood and cook for 4 minutes.

6. After 4 minutes, flip the dough, then spread the pizza sauce evenly over it. Sprinkle with the cheese, and top with the zucchini, onion, and pepper.

7. Close the hood and continue cooking for the remaining 2 to 3 minutes, until the cheese is melted and the veggie slices begin to crisp.

8. When cooking is complete, let cool slightly before slicing.

Per serving: *Calories: 554; Total fat: 22g; Saturated fat: 8g; Cholesterol: 30mg; Sodium: 1077mg; Carbohydrates: 71g; Fiber: 7g; Protein: 25g*

# Grilled Broccoli and Arugula Salad

**SERVES 4 / PREP TIME:** 10 MINUTES **/ TOTAL COOK TIME:** 12 MINUTES

*After an indulgent weekend, I crave a big bowl of greens and this salad definitely delivers. Each bite is bursting with peppery, earthy flavors, and the simple home-made lemon dressing adds a pop of brightness.*

GLUTEN-FREE, NUT-FREE, VEGETARIAN, UNDER 30 MINUTES

ACCESSORIES: Grill Grate

VARIATION TIP: Make this salad a complete meal by adding cooked lentils or quinoa in the final step.

**2 heads broccoli, trimmed into florets**

**½ red onion, sliced**

**1 tablespoon canola oil**

**2 tablespoons extra-virgin olive oil**

**1 tablespoon freshly squeezed lemon juice**

**1 teaspoon honey**

**1 teaspoon Dijon mustard**

**1 garlic clove, minced**

**Pinch red pepper flakes**

**¼ teaspoon fine sea salt**

**Freshly ground black pepper**

**4 cups arugula, torn**

**2 tablespoons grated Parmesan cheese**

1. Insert the Grill Grate and close the hood. Select GRILL, set the temperature to MAX, and set the time to 12 minutes. Select START/STOP to begin preheating.

2. While the unit is preheating, in a large bowl, combine the broccoli, sliced onions, and canola oil and toss until coated.

3. When the unit beeps to signify it has preheated, place the vegetables on the Grill Grate. Close the hood and grill for 8 to 12 minutes, until charred on all sides.

4. Meanwhile, in a medium bowl, whisk together the olive oil, lemon juice, honey, mustard, garlic, red pepper flakes, salt, and pepper.

5. When cooking is complete, combine the roasted vegetables and arugula in a large serving bowl. Drizzle with the vinaigrette to taste, and sprinkle with the Parmesan cheese.

*Per serving: Calories: 168; Total fat: 12g; Saturated fat: 2g; Cholesterol: 3mg; Sodium: 216mg; Carbohydrates: 13g; Fiber: 4g; Protein: 6g*

# Summary Vegetable Salad

**SERVES 4 / PREP TIME:** 10 MINUTES / **TOTAL COOK TIME:** 20 MINUTES

*In the summer months, my family always spends as much time as possible out-doors. From water activities on the lake to baseball games in the yard, we take advantage of every minute the sun is out. When the sun starts to set, we gather on the deck around the table. No matter what we are grilling for dinner, there is always a big platter of vegetables. With a variety of bright, charred flavors, this salad is inspired by that big platter. Like most of the recipes in this book, you can swap vegetables in and out based on what's in season and what you have on hand. Any combination is the right one.*

DAIRY-FREE, GLUTEN-FREE, NUT-FREE, VEGAN, UNDER 30 MINUTES

ACCESSORIES: Grill Grate

VARIATION TIP: I love the brightness a simple squeeze of lemon juice adds to this salad, but you can also use pesto or your favorite dressing to switch things up.

1 zucchini, sliced lengthwise about ¼-inch thick

1 summer squash, sliced lengthwise about ¼-inch thick

½ red onion, sliced

4 tablespoons canola oil, divided

2 portobello mushroom caps, trimmed with gills removed

2 ears corn, shucked

2 teaspoons freshly squeezed lemon juice

Sea salt

Freshly ground black pepper

1. Insert the Grill Grate and close the hood. Select GRILL, set the temperature to MAX, and set the time to 25 minutes. Select START/STOP to begin preheating.

2. Meanwhile, in a large bowl, toss the zucchini, squash, and onion with 2 tablespoons of oil until evenly coated.

3. When the unit beeps to signify it has preheated, arrange the zucchini, squash, and onions on the Grill Grate. Close the hood and cook for 6 minutes.

4. After 6 minutes, open the hood and flip the squash. Close the hood and cook for 6 to 9 minutes more.

5. Meanwhile, brush the mushrooms and corn with the remaining 2 tablespoons of oil.

CONTINUED ▶

6. When cooking is complete, remove the zucchini, squash, and onions and swap in the mushrooms and corn. Close the hood and cook for the remaining 10 minutes.

7. When cooking is complete, remove the mushrooms and corn, and let cool.

8. Cut the kernels from the cobs. Roughly chop all the vegetables into bite-size pieces.

9. Place the vegetables in a serving bowl and drizzle with lemon juice. Season with salt and pepper, and toss until evenly mixed.

*Per serving: Calories: 224; Total fat: 15g; Saturated fat: 1g; Cholesterol: 0mg; Sodium: 84mg; Carbohydrates: 22g; Fiber: 4g; Protein: 5g*

# Southwest Stuffed Peppers

**SERVES 6 / PREP TIME: 15 MINUTES / TOTAL COOK TIME: 32 MINUTES**

*Stuffed peppers are a go-to weeknight meal in our house because they're a simple, all-in-one meal that can be pulled together quickly. This version is vegetarian (omit the cheese to make them vegan), but it packs in a lot of protein thanks to the black beans! Top with fresh salsa and enjoy!*

GLUTEN-FREE, NUT-FREE, VEGETARIAN, FAMILY FAVORITE

ACCESSORIES: Grill Grate, Crisper Basked

- 6 red or green bell peppers, seeded, ribs removed, and top ½-inch cut off and reserved
- 4 garlic cloves, minced
- 1 small white onion, diced
- 2 (8.5-ounce) bags instant rice, cooked in microwave
- 1 (10-ounce) can red or green enchilada sauce
- ½ teaspoon chili powder
- ¼ teaspoon ground cumin
- ½ cup canned black beans, rinsed and drained
- ½ cup frozen corn
- ½ cup vegetable stock
- 1 (8-ounce) bag shredded Colby Jack cheese, divided

1. Chop the ½-inch portions of reserved bell pepper and place in a large mixing bowl. Add the garlic, onion, cooked instant rice, enchilada sauce, chili powder, cumin, black beans, corn, vegetable stock, and half the cheese. Mix to combine.

2. Use the cooking pot without the Grill Grate or Crisper Basket installed. Close the hood. Select ROAST, set the temperature to 350°F, and set the time to 32 minutes. Select START/STOP to begin preheating.

3. While the unit is preheating, spoon the mixture into the peppers, filling them up as full as possible. If necessary, lightly press the mixture down into the peppers to fit more in.

**4.** When the unit beeps to signify it has preheated, place the peppers, upright, in the pot. Close the hood and cook for 30 minutes.

**5.** After 30 minutes, sprinkle the remaining cheese over the top of the peppers. Close the hood and cook for the remaining 2 minutes.

**6.** When cooking is complete, serve immediately.

*Per serving: Calories: 328; Total Fat: 13g; Saturated Fat: 8g; Cholesterol: 33mg; Sodium: 417mg; Carbohydrates: 39g; Fiber: 4g; Protein: 13g*

# Portobello and Pesto Sliders

**SERVES 4 / PREP TIME:** 10 MINUTES **/ TOTAL COOK TIME:** 8 MINUTES

*One of the things I love most about Portobello mushrooms is their "meaty" factor. They are hearty and hold up well on the grill, making them a great veg- etarian burger alternative. The key to mushroom success is to enhance their flavor with a basic sauce or marinade, like balsamic vinegar, that plays up their earthy flavor. Whether you are looking for an easy weeknight meal or a way to sneak more veggies in at summer barbecues, these sliders are sure to fit the bill.*

NUT-FREE, VEGAN,
UNDER 30 MINUTES

ACCESSORIES: Grill Grate

DID YOU KNOW? Like many grilled vegetables, grilled mushrooms are best enjoyed the day they're made, but they can last for a few days in the refrigerator. If you have leftovers, cut them up and toss them into an omelet or frittata.

**8 small portobello mushrooms, trimmed with gills removed**

**2 tablespoons canola oil**

**2 tablespoons balsamic vinegar**

**8 slider buns**

**1 tomato, sliced**

**½ cup pesto**

**½ cup microgreens**

**1.** Insert the Grill Grate and close the hood. Select GRILL, set the temperature to HIGH, and set the time to 8 minutes. Select START/STOP to begin preheating.

**2.** While the unit is preheating, brush the mushrooms with the oil and balsamic vinegar.

**3.** When the unit beeps to signify it has preheated, place the mushrooms, gill-side down, on the Grill Grate. Close the hood and grill for 8 minutes, until the mushrooms are tender.

**4.** When cooking is complete, remove the mushrooms from the grill, and layer on the buns with tomato, pesto, and microgreens.

**Per serving:** *Calories: 373; Total fat: 22g; Saturated fat: 3g; Cholesterol: 8mg; Sodium: 442mg; Carbohydrates: 33g; Fiber: 4g; Protein: 12g*

# Cheesy Broccoli Calzones

**SERVES 4 / PREP TIME:** 10 MINUTES / **TOTAL COOK TIME:** 24 MINUTES

*Calzones are really just a fancy version of a giant pizza roll. You can customize the filling based on your preference or the ingredients you have on hand. This version is my personal favorite, but you can easily swap out the broccoli for another vegetable, like zucchini or mushrooms. You can also switch up the filling by stuffing them with cauliflower, buffalo sauce, and mozzarella (or, a more traditional pepperoni, pizza sauce, and mozzarella). Crispy on the outside and ooey-gooey on the inside, these calzones are sure to please no matter how you stuff them.*

NUT-FREE, VEGETARIAN, FAMILY FAVORITE

ACCESSORIES: Crisper Basket

VARIATION TIP: Make a double batch and freeze half of the calzones for quick dinners or lunch emergencies. Thaw to room temperature then reheat in the microwave or in a toaster oven at 300°F until heated through.

1 head broccoli, trimmed into florets

2 tablespoons extra-virgin olive oil

1 store-bought pizza dough (about 16 ounces)

2 to 3 tablespoons all-purpose flour, plus more for dusting

1 egg, beaten

2 cups shredded mozzarella cheese

1 cup ricotta cheese

½ cup grated Parmesan cheese

1 garlic clove, grated

Grated zest of 1 lemon

½ teaspoon red pepper flakes

Cooking oil spray

1. Insert the Crisper Basket and close the hood. Select AIR CRISP, set the temperature to 390°F, and set the time to 12 minutes. Select START/STOP to begin preheating.

2. Meanwhile, in a large bowl, toss the broccoli and olive oil until evenly coated.

3. When the unit beeps to signify it has preheated, add the broccoli to the basket. Close the hood and cook for 6 minutes.

CONTINUED ▶

4. While the broccoli is cooking, divide the pizza dough into four equal pieces. Dust a clean work surface with the flour. Place the dough on the floured surface, and roll each piece into an 8-inch round of even thickness. Dust your rolling pin and work surface with additional flour, as needed, to ensure the dough does not stick. Brush a thin coating of egg wash around the edges of each round.

5. After 6 minutes, shake the basket of broccoli. Place the basket back in the unit and close the hood to resume cooking.

6. Meanwhile, in a medium bowl, combine the mozzarella, ricotta, Parmesan cheese, garlic, lemon zest, and red pepper flakes.

7. After cooking is complete, add the broccoli to the cheese mixture. Spoon one-quarter of the mixture onto one side of each dough. Fold the other half over the filling, and press firmly to seal the edges together. Brush each calzone all over with the remaining egg wash.

8. Select AIR CRISP, set the temperature to 390°F, and set the time to 12 minutes. Select START/STOP to begin preheating.

9. When the unit beeps to signify it has preheated, coat the Crisper Basket with cooking spray and place the calzones in the basket. Cook for 10 to 12 minutes, until golden brown.

**Per serving:** Calories: 651; Total fat: 30g; Saturated fat: 13g; Cholesterol: 10mg; Sodium: 1083mg; Carbohydrates: 65g; Fiber: 7g; Protein: 38g

Seared Tuna Salad, *page 86*

# 6

# Fish and Seafood

# Seared Tuna Salad

**SERVES 4** / **PREP TIME:** 10 MINUTES / **TOTAL COOK TIME:** 6 MINUTES

*This is not your grandma's tuna salad. Put away the mayo and elevate your tuna salad game. While there's a time and place for canned tuna, this salad is built around perfectly grilled fresh ahi tuna. The Ninja® Foodi™ Grill's combination nonstick Grill Grate and super-heated air makes cooking fish a breeze, and you'll sear tuna like a pro. Try serving this salad at your next dinner party or with a glass of crisp white wine on a summer night.*

**DAIRY-FREE, GLUTEN-FREE, NUT-FREE, UNDER 30 MINUTES**

**ACCESSORIES:** Grill Grate

**HACK IT:** You can prepare the vinaigrette up to 3 days in advance. Store it in an airtight container in the refrigerator.

- **2 tablespoons rice wine vinegar**
- **¼ teaspoon sea salt, plus additional for seasoning**
- **½ teaspoon freshly ground black pepper, plus additional for seasoning**
- **6 tablespoons extra-virgin olive oil**
- **1 ½ pounds ahi tuna, cut into four strips**
- **2 tablespoons sesame oil**
- **1 (10-ounce) bag baby greens**
- **½ English cucumber, sliced**

1. Insert the Grill Grate, and close the hood. Select GRILL, set the temperature to MAX, and set the time to 6 minutes. Select START/STOP to begin preheating.

2. Meanwhile, in a small bowl, whisk together the rice vinegar, ¼ teaspoon of salt, and ½ teaspoon of pepper. Slowly pour in the oil while whisking, until the vinaigrette is fully combined.

3. Season the tuna with salt and pepper, and drizzle with the sesame oil.

**4.** When the unit beeps to signify it has preheated, place the tuna strips on the Grill Grate. Close the hood, and cook for 4 to 6 minutes. (There is no need to flip during cooking.)

**5.** While the tuna cooks, divide the baby greens and cucumber slices evenly among four plates or bowls.

**6.** When cooking is complete, top each salad with one tuna strip. Drizzle the vinaigrette over the top, and serve immediately.

*Per serving:* *Calories: 427; Total fat: 30g; Saturated fat: 4g; Cholesterol: 65mg; Sodium: 193mg; Carbohydrates: 5g; Fiber: 2g; Protein: 36g*

# Lemon-Garlic Shrimp Caesar Salad

**SERVES 4 / PREP TIME:** 10 MINUTES / **TOTAL COOK TIME:** 5 MINUTES

*In our house, one salad reigns supreme: the Caesar. My cookbooks include a number of different ways to put your own twist on the classic recipe. Here, I top the salad with citrusy jumbo shrimp, but you could easily swap out the shrimp for grilled chicken or salmon, if you prefer.*

GLUTEN-FREE, NUT-FREE, UNDER 30 MINUTES

ACCESSORIES: Grill Grate

VARIATION TIP: Elevate this salad even further by halving and grilling the heads of romaine before chopping and plating. Check out the Grilling Chart on page 189 for cook times.

**1 pound fresh jumbo shrimp**

**Juice of ½ lemon**

**3 garlic cloves, minced**

**Sea salt**

**Freshly ground black pepper**

**2 heads romaine lettuce, chopped**

**¾ cup Caesar dressing**

**½ cup grated Parmesan cheese**

1. Insert the Grill Grate and close the hood. Select GRILL, set the temperature to MAX, and set the time to 5 minutes. Select START/STOP to begin preheating.

2. In a large bowl, toss the shrimp with the lemon juice, garlic, salt, and pepper. Let marinate while the grill is preheating.

3. When the unit beeps to signify it has preheated, carefully place the shrimp on the Grill Grate. Close the hood and cook for 5 minutes. (There is no need to flip the shrimp during cooking.)

4. While the shrimp cooks, toss the romaine lettuce with the Caesar dressing, then divide evenly among four plates or bowls.

5. When cooking is complete, use tongs to remove the shrimp from the grill and place on top of each salad. Sprinkle with the Parmesan cheese and serve.

**Per serving:** *Calories: 279; Total fat: 11g; Saturated fat: 3g; Cholesterol: 232mg; Sodium: 789mg; Carbohydrates: 17g; Fiber: 2g; Protein: 30g*

# Spicy Shrimp Tacos

**SERVES 4 / PREP TIME:** 15 MINUTES / **TOTAL COOK TIME:** 10 MINUTES

*I was overwhelmed by the response to my Crispy Fish Taco recipe in* The Ninja® Foodi™ Complete Cookbook for Beginners. *So, when I first brought home the Foodi Grill, I knew I wanted to try a twist on that recipe by grilling the tortillas. That worked so well that I started experimenting with grilling proteins to stuff the tacos. Spicy shrimp was the favorite by far. The juxtaposition of spicy, juicy shrimp with cool, crunchy cabbage is the perfect combination for your next Taco Tuesday.*

**GLUTEN-FREE, NUT-FREE, UNDER 30 MINUTES, FAMILY FAVORITE**

**ACCESSORIES:** Grill Grate

**4 corn tortillas**

**Nonstick cooking spray**

**1 pound fresh jumbo shrimp**

**Juice of ½ lemon**

**1 teaspoon chili powder**

**1 teaspoon ground cumin**

**1 teaspoon Southwestern seasoning**

**¼ teaspoon cayenne pepper**

**2 cups shredded green cabbage**

**1 avocado, peeled and sliced**

1. Insert the Grill Grate and close the hood. Select GRILL, set the temperature to MAX, and set the time to 10 minutes. Select START/STOP to begin preheating.

2. While the unit is preheating, spray both sides of the tortillas with cooking spray, and in a large bowl, toss the shrimp with the lemon juice, chili powder, cumin, Southwestern seasoning, and cayenne pepper, until evenly coated. Let marinate while grilling the tortillas in the next step.

3. When the unit beeps to signify it has preheated, place 1 tortilla on the Grill Grate. Close the hood and grill for 1 minute. After 1 minute, open the hood and remove the tortilla; set aside. Repeat with the remaining 3 tortillas.

CONTINUED ▶

4. After removing the final tortilla, carefully place the shrimp on the Grill Grate. Close the hood and cook for 5 minutes. (There is no need to flip the shrimp during cooking.)

5. Remove the shrimp from the grill, arrange on the grilled tortillas, and top with cabbage and avocado. Feel free to include other toppings, such as cotija cheese, cilantro, and lime wedges.

*Per serving: Calories: 254; Total fat: 9g; Saturated fat: 2g; Cholesterol: 221mg; Sodium: 284mg; Carbohydrates: 17g; Fiber: 6g; Protein: 27g*

# Miso-Glazed Cod and Grilled Bok Choy

**SERVES 4 / PREP TIME:** 5 MINUTES, PLUS 30 MINUTES TO MARINATE
**TOTAL COOK TIME:** 17 MINUTES

*Most recipes for miso-glazed fish are for salmon; however, this version was inspired by the signature dish at a certain high-end restaurant known for marinating its cod in a miso glaze for a number of days. The miso marinade adds a salty sweetness to the buttery cod. The key is to marinate the fish for at least 30 minutes, but the longer you let the cod absorb the marinade, the deeper the flavor will be. This recipe is a great option for a weeknight meal, as it can be prepped over the weekend and left to marinate overnight.*

DAIRY-FREE, NUT-FREE

ACCESSORIES: Grill Grate

SUBSTITUTION TIP:
Mirin is a Japanese rice wine similar to sake. It pairs wonderfully with miso. Swap it in for the white wine used in the marinade in step 1.

**4 (6-ounce) cod fillets**

**¼ cup miso**

**3 tablespoons brown sugar**

**1 teaspoon sesame oil, divided**

**1 tablespoon white wine or mirin**

**2 tablespoons soy sauce**

**¼ teaspoon red pepper flakes**

**1 pound baby bok choy, halved lengthwise**

1. Place the cod, miso, brown sugar, ¾ teaspoon of sesame oil, and white wine in a large resealable plastic bag or container. Move the fillets around to coat evenly with the marinade. Refrigerate for 30 minutes.

2. Insert the Grill Grate and close the hood. Select GRILL, set the temperature to MAX, and set the time to 8 minutes. Select START/STOP to begin preheating.

3. When the unit beeps to signify it has preheated, place the fillets on the Grill Grate. Gently press them down to maximize grill marks. Close the hood and cook for 8 minutes. (There is no need to flip the fish during cooking.)

CONTINUED ▶

4. While the cod cooks, in a small bowl, whisk together the remaining ¼ teaspoon of sesame oil, soy sauce, and red pepper flakes. Brush the bok choy halves with the soy sauce mixture on all sides.

5. Remove the cod from the grill and set aside on a cutting board to rest. Tent with aluminum foil to keep warm.

6. Close the hood of the grill. Select GRILL, set the temperature to MAX, and set the time to 9 minutes. Select START/STOP to begin preheating to grill the bok choy.

7. When the unit beeps to signify it has preheated, place the bok choy on the Grill Grate, cut-side down. Close the hood and cook for 9 minutes. (There is no need to flip the bok choy during cooking.)

8. Remove the bok choy from the grill, plate with the cod, and serve.

**Per serving:** *Calories: 227; Total fat: 4g; Saturated fat: 0g; Cholesterol: 83mg; Sodium: 1273mg; Carbohydrates: 14g; Fiber: 2g; Protein: 34g*

# Honey-Lime Salmon with Avocado and Mango Salsa

**SERVES 4 / PREP TIME:** 10 MINUTES, PLUS 30 MINUTES TO MARINATE
**TOTAL COOK TIME:** 8 MINUTES

*One of the questions I always get asked is how to prepare fish at home. Almost every home cook I talk to is intimidated by cooking fish and opts to order it out instead. But grilling fish is one of the easiest and quickest ways to prepare it, and salmon is a perfect place to start. This recipe is a flavor explosion in all the best ways. The marinade on the buttery salmon is sweet and tart from the honey and lime. When grilled, the honey caramelizes, intensifying the flavor and creating a crisp crust. The fresh salsa pulls the dish together, with bright citrus and heat from the jalapeño.*

NUT-FREE

ACCESSORIES: Grill Grate

HACK IT: Refrigerate any leftover salsa and use it on top of grilled chicken or tacos, or serve it with your favorite tortilla chips.

- 2 tablespoons unsalted butter, melted
- ⅓ cup honey
- 1 tablespoon soy sauce
- Juice of 3 limes, divided
- Grated zest of ½ lime
- 3 garlic cloves, minced and divided
- 4 (6-ounce) skinless salmon fillets
- 1 mango, peeled and diced
- 1 avocado, peeled and diced
- ½ tomato, diced
- ½ red onion, diced
- 1 jalapeño pepper, seeded, stemmed, and diced
- 1 tablespoon extra-virgin olive oil
- Sea salt
- Freshly ground black pepper

1. Place the butter, honey, soy sauce, juice of 2 limes, lime zest, and 2 minced garlic cloves in a large resealable plastic bag or container. Add the salmon fillets and coat evenly with the marinade. Refrigerate for 30 minutes.

2. While the salmon is marinating, in a large bowl, combine the mango, avocado, tomato, onion, remaining minced garlic clove, jalapeño, remaining juice of 1 lime, oil, salt, and pepper. Cover and refrigerate.

CONTINUED ▶

3. Insert the Grill Grate and close the hood. Select GRILL, set the temperature to MAX, and set the time to 8 minutes. Select START/STOP to begin preheating.

4. When the unit beeps to signify it has preheated, place the fillets on the Grill Grate, gently pressing them down to maximize grill marks. Close the hood and cook for 6 minutes. (There is no need to flip the fish during cooking.)

5. After 6 minutes, check the fillets for doneness; the internal temperature should read at least 140°F on a food thermometer. If necessary, close the hood and continue cooking up to 2 minutes more.

6. When cooking is complete, top the fillets with salsa and serve immediately.

*Per serving: Calories: 892; Total fat: 57g; Saturated fat: 15g; Cholesterol: 161mg; Sodium: 465mg; Carbohydrates: 49g; Fiber: 37g; Protein: 51g*

# Spicy Sriracha-Glazed Salmon

**SERVES 4 / PREP TIME:** 10 MINUTES, PLUS 30 MINUTES TO MARINATE
**TOTAL COOK TIME:** 8 MINUTES

*With just five ingredients and less than 10 minutes on the Ninja® Foodi™ Grill, this simple salmon recipe is the ultimate weeknight dinner. And when I say simple, I really mean simple! No flipping required. Marinated in a sweet and spicy honey-sriracha sauce, these salmon fillets are great served over white rice and with a big helping of Grilled Asian-Style Broccoli (page 52).*

**DAIRY-FREE, GLUTEN-FREE, NUT-FREE, 5-INGREDIENT**

**ACCESSORIES:** Grill Grate

**DID YOU KNOW?** The Ninja Foodi Grill makes quick work of frozen fish, transforming it from frozen to char-grilled in minutes. If you're using frozen salmon in this recipe, increase the cook time to 10 to 13 minutes.

1 cup sriracha

Juice of 2 lemons

¼ cup honey

4 (6-ounce) skinless salmon fillets

Chives, chopped, for garnish

1. Place the sriracha, lemon juice, and honey in a large resealable plastic bag or container. Add the salmon fillets and coat evenly. Refrigerate for 30 minutes.

2. Insert the Grill Grate and close the hood. Select GRILL, set the temperature to MAX, and set the time to 8 minutes. Select START/STOP to begin preheating.

3. When the unit beeps to signify it has preheated, place the fillets on the Grill Grate, gently pressing them down to maximize grill marks. Close the hood and cook for 6 minutes. (There is no need to flip the fish during cooking.)

4. After 6 minutes, check the fillets for doneness; the internal temperature should read at least 140°F on a food thermometer. If necessary, close the hood and continue cooking up to 2 minutes more.

5. When cooking is complete, remove the fillets from the grill. Plate, and garnish with the chives.

**Per serving:** *Calories: 507; Total fat: 27g; Saturated fat: 7g; Cholesterol: 94mg; Sodium: 511mg; Carbohydrates: 33g; Fiber: 1g; Protein: 32g*

# Grilled Swordfish in Caper Sauce

**SERVES 4 / PREP TIME:** 5 MINUTES, PLUS 15 MINUTES TO MARINATE
**TOTAL COOK TIME:** 8 MINUTES

*Swordfish is a great choice for grilling because its firm, lean flesh is hearty and holds up well on the grill. It's perfect for a quick weeknight meal, but also a surefire way to impress your guests at your next dinner party. The lemony caper sauce offers a brightness to the dish that is the perfect contrast to the smoky meatiness of the swordfish. Once your fish is off the grill, toss some asparagus right on the Grill Grate and you'll have a full meal in minutes.*

GLUTEN-FREE, NUT-FREE, UNDER 30 MINUTES

ACCESSORIES: Grill Grate

DID YOU KNOW? If you are looking for a wine pairing for swordfish, choose a white wine that is on the richer side, like a Sauvignon Blanc or Chardonnay.

1 tablespoon freshly squeezed lemon juice

1 tablespoon extra-virgin olive oil

Sea salt

Freshly ground black pepper

4 fresh (8-ounce) swordfish steaks, about 1-inch thick

4 tablespoons unsalted butter

1 lemon, sliced crosswise into 8 slices

2 tablespoons capers, drained

1. In a large shallow bowl, whisk together the lemon juice and oil. Season the swordfish steaks with salt and pepper on each side, and place them in the oil mixture. Turn to coat both sides. Refrigerate for 15 minutes.

2. Insert the Grill Grate and close the hood. Select GRILL, set the temperature to MAX, and set the time to 8 minutes. Select START/STOP to begin preheating.

3. When the unit beeps to signify it has preheated, place the swordfish on the Grill Grate. Close the hood and cook for 9 minutes. (There is no need to flip the swordfish during cooking.)

**4.** While the swordfish cooks, melt the butter in a small saucepan over medium heat. Stir and cook for about 3 minutes, until the butter has slightly browned. Add the lemon slices and capers to the pan, and cook for 1 minute. Turn off the heat.

**5.** Remove the swordfish from the grill and transfer it to a cutting board. Slice the fish into thick strips, transfer to serving platter, pour the caper sauce over the top, and serve immediately.

**Per serving:** *Calories: 472; Total fat: 31g; Saturated fat: 8g; Cholesterol: 31mg; Sodium: 269mg; Carbohydrates: 2g; Fiber: 1g; Protein: 48g*

# New England Fish Sandwich

**SERVES 4 / PREP TIME:** 10 MINUTES / **TOTAL COOK TIME:** 15 MINUTES

*The New England fried fish sandwich is a staple of the eastern coast of the United States, and living in Boston, we are privy to some of the best seafood restaurants and clam shacks in the area. The perfect fish sandwich is light and crispy on the outside, and super moist and flaky on the inside. Cod and haddock are the most common fish used for frying and are interchangeable in this recipe. Served up with tartar sauce on a fresh roll, this sandwich is so good, it rivals some of the best seafood restaurants on the East Coast, if I do say so myself.*

NUT-FREE, UNDER
30 MINUTES, FAMILY
FAVORITE

**ACCESSORIES:** Crisper
Basket

**VARIATION TIP:** Want a
different kind of crunch?
Swap out the lettuce
for a simple slaw made
with sliced red cabbage,
grated carrots, red wine
vinegar, and extra-virgin
olive oil.

2 large eggs

10 ounces beer (an ale,
IPA, or any type you
have on hand will work)

1½ teaspoons hot sauce

1½ cups cornstarch

1½ cups all-purpose flour

1 teaspoon sea salt

1 teaspoon freshly
ground black pepper

4 fresh (5- or 6-ounce)
cod fillets

Nonstick cooking spray

4 soft rolls, sliced

Tartar sauce

Lettuce leaves

Lemon wedges

**1.** Insert the Crisper Basket and close the hood. Select AIR CRISP, set the temperature to 375ºF, and set the time to 15 minutes. Select START/STOP to begin preheating.

**2.** While the unit is preheating, whisk together the eggs, beer, and hot sauce in a large shallow bowl. In a separate large bowl, whisk together the cornstarch, flour, salt, and pepper.

**3.** One at a time, coat the cod fillets in the egg mixture, then dredge them in the flour mixture and coat on all sides. Repeat with the remaining cod fillets.

CONTINUED ▶

**4.** When the unit beeps to signify it has preheated, spray the Crisper Basket with the cooking spray. Place the fish fillets in the basket and coat them with the cooking spray. Close the hood and cook for 15 minutes.

**5.** After 15 minutes, check the fish for desired crispiness. Remove from the basket.

**6.** Assemble the sandwiches by spreading tartar sauce on one half of each of the sliced rolls. Add one fish fillet and lettuce leaves, and serve with lemon wedges.

Per serving: Calories: 509; Total fat: 9g; Saturated fat: 1g; Cholesterol: 169mg; Sodium: 1119mg; Carbohydrates: 62g; Fiber: 2g; Protein: 40g

# Crab Cakes with Cajun Aioli

**SERVES 4 / PREP TIME:** 10 MINUTES **/ TOTAL COOK TIME:** 10 MINUTES

*Call me crazy, but I think that crab should be the primary flavor in crab cakes. If you agree, you'll love this recipe for crab cakes full of meaty crab chunks. But what puts these crab cakes over the top is the Cajun aioli for dipping. Serve with homemade slaw or a warm potato salad. You can also turn these crab cakes into a tasty sandwich by serving them on your favorite rolls topped with the aioli.*

**DAIRY-FREE, UNDER 30 MINUTES**

**ACCESSORIES:** Crisper Basket

**DID YOU KNOW?** If you are preparing meals for the week ahead or making these crab cakes for a party, you can prepare the crab mixture and patties 1 or 2 days in advance. Just store them in an airtight container in the refrigerator.

- 1 egg
- ½ cup mayonnaise, plus 3 tablespoons
- Juice of ½ lemon
- 1 tablespoon minced scallions (green parts only)
- 1 teaspoon Old Bay seasoning
- 8 ounces lump crabmeat
- ⅓ cup bread crumbs
- Nonstick cooking spray
- ½ teaspoon cayenne pepper
- ¼ teaspoon paprika
- ¼ teaspoon garlic powder
- ¼ teaspoon chili powder
- ¼ teaspoon onion powder
- ¼ teaspoon freshly ground black pepper
- ⅛ teaspoon ground nutmeg

1. Insert the Crisper Basket and close the hood. Select AIR CRISP, set the temperature to 375°F, and set the time to 10 minutes. Select START/STOP to begin preheating.

2. While the unit is preheating, in a medium bowl, whisk together the egg, 3 tablespoons of mayonnaise, lemon juice, scallions, and Old Bay seasoning. Gently stir in the crabmeat, making sure not to break up the meat into small pieces. Add the bread crumbs, and gradually mix them in. Form the mixture into four patties.

3. When the unit beeps to signify it has preheated, place the crab cakes in the basket and coat them with the cooking spray. Close the hood and cook for 10 minutes.

CONTINUED ▶

**4.** While the crab cakes are cooking, in a small bowl, mix the remaining ½ cup of mayonnaise, cayenne pepper, paprika, garlic powder, chili powder, onion powder, black pepper, and nutmeg until fully combined.

**5.** When cooking is complete, serve the crab cakes with the Cajun aioli spooned on top.

*Per serving:* *Calories: 347; Total fat: 34g; Saturated fat: 5g; Cholesterol: 87mg; Sodium: 812mg; Carbohydrates: 9g; Fiber: 1g; Protein: 11g*

# Coconut Shrimp

**SERVES 4** / **PREP TIME:** 15 MINUTES / **TOTAL COOK TIME:** 15 MINUTES

*Crisped to perfection in the Ninja® Foodi™ Grill, these coconut air-fried shrimp are downright addictive. These tasty little bites are crunchy on the outside and tender on the inside. You won't believe how quick and easy these restaurant-style shrimp are to make at home! If you need a crowd-pleasing appetizer, these are a must. Or, serve them with a side of fluffy rice or a simple green salad.*

**DAIRY-FREE, NUT-FREE, UNDER 30 MINUTES**

**ACCESSORIES:** Crisper Basket

- ½ **cup all-purpose flour**
- 2 **teaspoons freshly ground black pepper**
- ½ **teaspoon sea salt**
- 2 **large eggs**
- ¾ **cup unsweetened coconut flakes**
- ¼ **cup panko bread crumbs**
- 24 **peeled, deveined shrimp**
- **Nonstick cooking spray**
- **Sweet chili sauce, for serving**

1. Insert the Crisper Basket and close the hood. Select AIR CRISP, set the temperature to 400°F, and set the time to 8 minutes. Select START/STOP to begin preheating.

2. While the unit is preheating, in a medium shallow bowl, mix together the flour, black pepper, and salt. In a second medium shallow bowl, whisk the eggs. In a third, combine the coconut flakes and bread crumbs.

3. Dredge each shrimp in the flour mixture, then in the egg. Press each shrimp into the coconut mixture on both sides, leaving the tail uncoated.

4. When the unit beeps to signify it has preheated, place half of the shrimp into the basket and coat them with the cooking spray. Close the hood and cook for 7 minutes.

CONTINUED ▶

5. Remove the cooked shrimp and add the remaining uncooked shrimp to the basket. Spray them with the cooking spray, close the hood, and cook for 7 minutes.

6. Serve with sweet chili sauce.

*Per serving: Calories: 342; Total fat: 14g; Saturated fat: 10g; Cholesterol: 262mg; Sodium: 451mg; Carbohydrates: 23g; Fiber: 4g; Protein: 30g*

# Classic Crispy Fish Sticks

**SERVES 4 / PREP TIME:** 10 MINUTES / **TOTAL COOK TIME:** 10 MINUTES

*This classic fish stick recipe is an update on the traditional store-bought frozen fish we all loved growing up. This version is made with a handful of simple ingredients, so you know exactly what is in every bite. Whether you're making a batch for the kids or for yourself, these tasty fish sticks are perfect for the whole family. Serve with your favorite dipping sauce—I love a simple lemon aioli.*

**DAIRY-FREE, NUT-FREE, UNDER 30 MINUTES, FAMILY FAVORITE**

**ACCESSORIES:** Crisper Basket

**DID YOU KNOW?** These fish sticks can be made ahead and frozen, so you can enjoy them anytime. Simply place them on a plate or a baking sheet with plenty of space in between so they don't stick together. Once frozen, place them in an airtight container or resealable bag in the freezer. When properly stored, they can last 2 or 3 months in the freezer.

1 pound cod fillets

¼ cup all-purpose flour

1 large egg

1 teaspoon Dijon mustard

½ cup bread crumbs

1 tablespoon dried parsley

1 teaspoon paprika

½ teaspoon freshly ground black pepper

Nonstick cooking spray

1. Insert the Crisper Basket, and close the hood. Select AIR CRISP, set the temperature to 390°F, and set the time to 10 minutes. Select START/STOP to begin preheating.

2. While the unit is preheating, cut the fish fillets into ¾- to 1-inch-wide strips.

3. Place the flour on a plate. In a medium shallow bowl, whisk together the egg and Dijon mustard. In a separate medium shallow bowl, combine the bread crumbs, dried parsley, paprika, and black pepper.

4. One at a time, dredge the cod strips in the flour, shaking off any excess, then coat them in the egg mixture. Finally, dredge them in the bread crumb mixture, and coat on all sides.

5. When the unit beeps to signify it has preheated, spray the basket with the cooking spray. Place the cod fillet strips in the basket, and coat them with the cooking spray. Close the hood, and cook for 10 minutes.

6. Remove the fish sticks from the basket and serve.

*Per serving:* **Per serving:** *Calories: 191; Total fat: 3g; Saturated fat: 1g; Cholesterol: 96mg; Sodium: 199mg; Carbohydrates: 16g; Fiber: 1g; Protein: 24g*

**Greek Chicken and Veggie Kebabs,** *page 112*

# 7

# Poultry

# Greek Chicken and Veggie Kebabs

**SERVES 4 / PREP TIME:** 15 MINUTES, PLUS 30 MINUTES TO MARINATE
**TOTAL COOK TIME:** 14 MINUTES

*There is something inherently fun about kebabs. Whether you're whipping up these Greek Chicken and Veggie Kebabs or my Teriyaki Chicken and Pineapple Kebabs (page 114), I just think everything is better bite-size. Maybe it's because the marinade covers every nook and cranny? Or, maybe it's because they're easy to eat with your hands? Serve these kebabs with a side of tzatziki for dipping, and enjoy as a light dinner or fun snack.*

GLUTEN-FREE, NUT-FREE

ACCESSORIES: Grill Grate, Ninja® Foodi™ Grill Kebab Skewers, or wood skewers

DID YOU KNOW? I always recommend letting protein marinate for at least 30 minutes, but the longer it marinates, the better the flavor will be. I often prep marinated proteins, like the chicken in this recipe, the night before. This cuts down on prep time when cooking and ensures that flavor builds for almost 24 hours. Alternatively, save even more time by prepping the whole recipe, place the pre-made skewers in a plastic bag or container, and refrigerate.

2 tablespoons plain Greek yogurt

¼ cup extra-virgin olive oil

Juice of 4 lemons

Grated zest of 1 lemon

4 garlic cloves, minced

2 tablespoons dried oregano

1 teaspoon sea salt

½ teaspoon freshly ground black pepper

1 pound boneless, skinless chicken breasts, cut into 2-inch cubes

1 red onion, quartered

1 zucchini, sliced

1. In a large bowl, whisk together the Greek yogurt, oil, lemon juice, zest, garlic, oregano, salt, and pepper until well combined.

2. Place the chicken and half of the marinade into a large resealable plastic bag or container. Move the chicken around to coat evenly. Refrigerate for at least 30 minutes.

3. Insert the Grill Grate and close the hood. Select GRILL, set the temperature to MEDIUM, and set the time to 14 minutes. Select START/STOP to begin preheating.

4. While the unit is preheating, assemble the kebabs by threading the chicken on the skewers, alternating with the red onion and zucchini. Ensure the ingredients are pushed almost completely down to the end of the skewers.

5. When the unit beeps to signify it has preheated, place the skewers on the Grill Grate. Close hood and cook for 10 to 14 minutes, occasionally basting the kebabs with the remaining marinade while cooking.

6. Cooking is complete when the internal temperature of the chicken reaches 165ºF on a food thermometer.

**Per serving:** *Calories: 283; Total fat: 16g; Saturated fat: 2g; Cholesterol: 72mg; Sodium: 545mg; Carbohydrates: 8g; Fiber: 2g; Protein: 26g*

# Teriyaki Chicken and Pineapple Kebabs

**SERVES 4 / PREP TIME:** 15 MINUTES, PLUS 30 MINUTES TO MARINATE
**TOTAL COOK TIME:** 14 MINUTES

*This combination of sticky, sweet teriyaki and fresh pineapple is made even more delicious by the Ninja® Foodi™ Grill. The heat caramelizes the teriyaki-marinated chicken, so it's tender on the inside and crisp on the outside. At the same time, the sugars in the pineapple are intensified and become almost smoky. Just four simple ingredients and a few minutes on the grill, and this blend of citrusy-spiced flavors will transport you right to a sunny beach. Enjoy these kebabs as-is, or remove the meat and vegetables and serve atop a bed of rice.*

**DAIRY-FREE, NUT-FREE, 5-INGREDIENT**

**ACCESSORIES:** Grill Grate, Ninja Foodi Grill Kebab Skewers, or wood skewers

**SUBSTITUTION TIP:** Pre-made teriyaki sauce is quick and convenient. If you prefer to use a homemade teriyaki sauce to pack even more punch, use the same amount as indicated in the recipe.

1 pound boneless, skinless chicken breasts, cut into 2-inch cubes

1 cup teriyaki sauce, divided

2 green bell peppers, seeded and cut into 1-inch cubes

2 cups fresh pineapple, cut into 1-inch cubes

1. Place the chicken and ½ cup of teriyaki sauce in a large resealable plastic bag or container. Toss to coat evenly. Refrigerate for at least 30 minutes.

2. Insert the Grill Grate and close the hood. Select GRILL, set the temperature to MEDIUM, and set the time to 14 minutes. Select START/STOP to begin preheating.

3. While the unit is preheating, assemble the kebabs by threading the chicken onto the skewers, alternating with the peppers and pineapple. Ensure the ingredients are pushed almost completely down to the end of the skewers.

**4.** When the unit beeps to signify it has preheated, place the skewers on the Grill Grate. Close the hood and cook for 10 to 14 minutes, occasionally basting the kebabs with the remaining ½ cup of teriyaki sauce while cooking.

**5.** Cooking is complete when the internal temperature of the chicken reaches 165ºF on a food thermometer.

*Per serving:* *Calories: 252; Total fat: 3g; Saturated fat: 0g; Cholesterol: 72mg; Sodium: 2819mg; Carbohydrates: 27g; Fiber: 2g; Protein: 29g*

# Fajita-Style Chicken Kebabs

**SERVES 4 / PREP TIME:** 15 MINUTES, PLUS 30 MINUTES TO MARINATE
**TOTAL COOK TIME:** 14 MINUTES

*I love when a meal gets the whole gang involved. There is a special bond formed when family or friends cook together and can tailor a recipe to their liking. Fajita night has always been a favorite in our house and this recipe offers a fun twist. My husband Julien and I prep the veggies and thread the kebabs, loading up on our favorite ingredients. My kebabs are always heavy on the onion, while Julien doubles the amount of chicken to veggies. It's a fun way to spend time together and make a delicious meal.*

**DAIRY-FREE, GLUTEN-FREE, NUT-FREE**

**ACCESSORIES:** Grill Grate and Ninja® Foodi™ Grill Kebab Skewers (or wood skewers)

**DID YOU KNOW?** If you're using wood or bamboo skewers, always soak the skewers for at least 30 minutes before using them on the grill. This will ensure they do not dry out and break while grilling.

1 tablespoon ground cumin

1 tablespoon garlic powder

1 tablespoon chili powder

2 teaspoons paprika

¼ teaspoon sea salt

¼ teaspoon freshly ground black pepper

1 pound boneless, skinless chicken breasts, cut in 2-inch cubes

2 tablespoons extra-virgin olive oil, divided

2 red bell peppers, seeded and cut into 1-inch cubes

1 red onion, quartered

Juice of 1 lime

1. In a small mixing bowl, combine the cumin, garlic powder, chili powder, paprika, salt, and pepper, and mix well.

2. Place the chicken, 1 tablespoon oil, and half of the spice mixture into a large resealable plastic bag or container. Toss to coat evenly.

3. Place the bell pepper, onion, remaining 1 tablespoon of oil, and remaining spice mixture into a large resealable plastic bag or container. Toss to coat evenly. Refrigerate the chicken and vegetables for at least 30 minutes.

4. Insert the Grill Grate and close the hood. Select GRILL, set the temperature to HIGH, and set the time to 14 minutes. Select START/STOP to begin preheating.

**5.** While the unit is preheating, assemble the kebabs by threading the chicken onto the skewers, alternating with the peppers and onion. Ensure the ingredients are pushed almost completely down to the end of the skewers.

**6.** When the unit beeps to signify it has preheated, place the skewers on the Grill Grate. Close the hood and cook for 10 to 14 minutes.

**7.** Cooking is complete when the internal temperature of the chicken reaches 165ºF. When cooking is complete, remove from the heat, and drizzle with lime juice.

**Per serving:** *Calories: 231; Total fat: 11g; Saturated fat: 1g; Cholesterol: 72mg; Sodium: 198mg; Carbohydrates: 9g; Fiber: 2g; Protein: 25g*

# Lemon and Fresh Herb Grilled Chicken Thighs

**SERVES 4 / PREP TIME:** 10 MINUTES, PLUS 30 MINUTES TO MARINATE
**TOTAL COOK TIME:** 13 MINUTES

*The beauty of grilling is that it elevates even the simplest of ingredients. I love this recipe because it celebrates a handful of inexpensive, unassuming ingredients. Serve alongside Bacon Brussels Sprouts (page 51) or Garlicky Summer Squash and Charred Red Onion (page 54).*

DAIRY-FREE, GLUTEN-FREE, NUT-FREE

ACCESSORIES: Grill Grate

DID YOU KNOW? This recipe will cook up deliciously moist and perfectly charred chicken thighs without the need to flip the meat. But if you want to create a platter that boasts telltale grill marks, as we did here, flip the thighs halfway through cooking.

Grated zest of 2 lemons

Juice of 2 lemons

3 sprigs fresh rosemary, leaves finely chopped

3 sprigs fresh sage, leaves finely chopped

2 garlic cloves, minced

¼ teaspoon red pepper flakes

¼ cup canola oil

Sea salt

4 (4- to 7-ounce) boneless chicken thighs

1. In a small bowl, whisk together the lemon zest and juice, rosemary, sage, garlic, red pepper flakes, and oil. Season with salt.

2. Place the chicken and lemon-herb mixture in a large resealable plastic bag or container. Toss to coat evenly. Refrigerate the chicken for at least 30 minutes.

3. Insert the Grill Grate and close the hood. Select GRILL, set the temperature to HIGH, and set the time to 13 minutes. Select START/STOP to begin preheating.

4. When the unit beeps to signify it has preheated, place the chicken on the Grill Grate. Close the hood and cook for 10 to 13 minutes.

5. Cooking is complete when the internal temperature of the chicken reaches at least 165°F on a food thermometer.

*Per serving: Calories: 486; Total fat: 39g; Saturated fat: 9g; Cholesterol: 143mg; Sodium: 189mg; Carbohydrates: 1g; Fiber: 0g; Protein: 30g*

# Zesty Garlic Grilled Chicken

**SERVES 4 / PREP TIME:** 5 MINUTES, PLUS 30 MINUTES TO MARINATE
**TOTAL COOK TIME:** 18 MINUTES

*This grilled chicken is wonderfully versatile and so easy to make ahead. In our case, we prep this recipe over the weekend and turn the chicken into a number of different meals to enjoy throughout the week. I serve this zesty chicken over rice and beans for burrito bowls at lunch, enjoy it with char-grilled corn tortillas for a satisfying Taco Tuesday, or toss it with romaine, tomatoes, corn, and a creamy dressing for a light dinner.*

DAIRY-FREE, GLUTEN-FREE, NUT-FREE, FAMILY FAVORITE, 5-INGREDIENT

ACCESSORIES: Grill Grate

1½ tablespoons extra-virgin olive oil

3 garlic cloves, minced

¼ teaspoon ground cumin

Sea salt

Freshly ground black pepper

Grated zest of 1 lime

Juice of 1 lime

4 boneless, skinless chicken breasts

1. In a large shallow bowl, stir together the oil, garlic, cumin, salt, pepper, zest, and lime juice. Add the chicken breasts and coat well. Cover and marinate in the refrigerator for 30 minutes.

2. Insert the Grill Grate and close the hood. Select GRILL, set the temperature to MEDIUM, and set the time to 18 minutes. Select START/STOP to begin preheating.

3. When the unit has beeped to signify it has preheated, place the chicken breasts on the Grill Grate. Close the hood and cook for 7 minutes. After 7 minutes, flip the chicken, close the hood, and cook for an additional 7 minutes.

CONTINUED ▶

4. Check the chicken for doneness. If needed, cook up to 4 minutes more. Cooking is complete when the internal temperature of the chicken reaches at least 165°F on a food thermometer.

5. Remove from the grill, and place on a cutting board or platter to rest for 5 minutes. Serve.

**Per serving:** *Calories: 169; Total fat: 7g; Saturated fat: 1g; Cholesterol: 65mg; Sodium: 134mg; Carbohydrates: 1g; Fiber: 0g; Protein: 26g*

# Honey-Sriracha Grilled Chicken Thighs

**SERVES 4 / PREP TIME:** 5 MINUTES, PLUS 30 MINUTES TO MARINATE / **TOTAL COOK TIME:** 17 MINUTES

*Sweet and spicy, this recipe is packed with flavor, despite only using four ingredients! The sticky glaze reminds me of the best Chinese takeout recipes, without all the guilt of lots of fat and calories. Serve on top of white rice with a side of Blistered Green Beans (page 49).*

**DAIRY-FREE, GLUTEN-FREE, NUT-FREE, FAMILY FAVORITE, 5-INGREDIENT**

**ACCESSORIES:** Grill Grate

1 cup sriracha

Juice of 2 lemons

¼ cup honey

4 bone-in chicken thighs

1. Place the sriracha, lemon juice, and honey in a large resealable plastic bag or container. Add the chicken thighs and toss to coat evenly. Refrigerate for 30 minutes.

2. Insert the Grill Grate and close the hood. Select GRILL, set the temperature to MEDIUM, and set the time to 14 minutes. Select START/STOP to begin preheating.

3. When the unit beeps to signify it has preheated, place the chicken thighs onto the Grill Grate, gently pressing them down to maximize grill marks. Close the hood and cook for 7 minutes.

4. After 7 minutes, flip the chicken thighs using tongs. Close the hood and cook for 7 minutes more.

5. Cooking is complete when the internal temperature of the meat reaches at least 165°F on a food thermometer. If necessary, close the hood and continue cooking for 2 to 3 minutes more.

6. When cooking is complete, remove the chicken from the grill, and let it rest for 5 minutes before serving.

*Per serving: Calories: 484; Total fat: 26g; Saturated fat: 8g; Cholesterol: 143mg; Sodium: 548mg; Carbohydrates: 30g; Fiber: 0g; Protein: 30g*

# Maple-Glazed Chicken Wings

**SERVES 4 / PREP TIME:** 5 MINUTES / **TOTAL COOK TIME:** 14 MINUTES

*Grilled chicken wings are vastly different from the traditional fried wings. It's all about building texture and flavor. Unlike other cuts of chicken, there's no need to marinate the wings first because they stay moist while cooking. Alternatively, you can skip the glaze and serve the wings plain with the sauce on the side.*

**DAIRY-FREE, NUT-FREE, UNDER 30 MINUTES, FAMILY FAVORITE**

**ACCESSORIES:** Grill Grate

**VARIATION TIP:** Spice up this maple-glazed wing recipe by adding ¼ teaspoon red pepper flakes to the maple syrup mixture.

1 cup maple syrup

⅓ cup soy sauce

¼ cup teriyaki sauce

3 garlic cloves, minced

2 teaspoons garlic powder

2 teaspoons onion powder

1 teaspoon freshly ground black pepper

2 pounds bone-in chicken wings (drumettes and flats)

1. Insert the Grill Grate and close the hood. Select GRILL, set the temperature to MEDIUM, and set the time to 14 minutes. Select START/STOP to begin preheating.

2. Meanwhile, in a large bowl, whisk together the maple syrup, soy sauce, teriyaki sauce, garlic, garlic powder, onion powder, and black pepper. Add the wings, and use tongs to toss and coat.

3. When the unit has beeped to signify it has preheated, place the chicken wings on the Grill Grate. Close the hood and cook for 5 minutes. After 5 minutes, flip the wings, close the hood, and cook for an additional 5 minutes.

4. Check the wings for doneness. Cooking is complete when the internal temperature of the meat reaches at least 165°F on a food thermometer. If needed, cook for up to 4 minutes more.

5. Remove from the grill and serve.

*Per serving: Calories: 722; Total fat: 36g; Saturated fat: 10g; Cholesterol: 230mg; Sodium: 2096mg; Carbohydrates: 59g; Fiber: 1g; Protein: 41g*

# Dill Pickle Chicken Wings

**SERVES 4 / PREP TIME:** 5 MINUTES, PLUS 2 HOURS TO MARINATE
**TOTAL COOK TIME:** 26 MINUTES

*These Dill Pickle Chicken Wings are tender, juicy, and just plain delicious. Not to mention a nice change of pace from traditional buffalo chicken wings. The secret to these wings is to brine them in dill pickle juice before they cook. The pickle juice tenderizes the chicken, and the Ninja® Foodi™ Grill crisps the wings to perfection. Serve with creamy ranch dressing—and maybe a few pickles, too.*

DAIRY-FREE, GLUTEN-FREE, NUT-FREE, 5-INGREDIENT

ACCESSORIES: Crisper Basket

**VARIATION TIP:** For classic buffalo chicken wings, follow the cook time for this recipe but skip the marinade and seasoning. Once the wings are cooked and crispy, toss them with a few tablespoons of buffalo sauce.

**2 pounds bone-in chicken wings (drumettes and flats)**

**1½ cups dill pickle juice**

**1½ tablespoons vegetable oil**

**½ tablespoon dried dill**

**¾ teaspoon garlic powder**

**Sea salt**

**Freshly ground black pepper**

1. Place the chicken wings in a large shallow bowl. Pour the pickle juice over the top, ensuring all of the wings are coated and as submerged as possible. Cover and refrigerate for 2 hours.

2. Insert the Crisper Basket and close the hood. Select AIR CRISP, set the temperature to 390°F, and set the time to 26 minutes. Select START/STOP to begin preheating.

3. While the unit is preheating, rinse the brined chicken wings under cool water, then pat them dry with a paper towel. Place in a large bowl.

4. In a small bowl, whisk together the oil, dill, garlic powder, salt, and pepper. Drizzle over the wings and toss to fully coat them.

**5.** When the unit beeps to signify it has preheated, place the wings in the basket, spreading them out evenly. Close the hood and cook for 11 minutes.

**6.** After 11 minutes, flip the wings with tongs. Close the hood and cook for 11 minutes more.

**7.** Check the wings for doneness. Cooking is complete when the internal temperature of the chicken reaches at least 165°F on a food thermometer. If needed, cook for up to 4 more minutes.

**8.** Remove the wings from the basket and serve immediately.

**Per serving:** *Calories: 529; Total fat: 41g; Saturated fat: 10g; Cholesterol: 230mg; Sodium: 347mg; Carbohydrates: 1g; Fiber: 0g; Protein: 38g*

# Spicy Barbecue Chicken Drumsticks

**SERVES 4 / PREP TIME:** 10 MINUTES / **TOTAL COOK TIME:** 20 MINUTES

*A chicken leg has two parts: the drumstick and the thigh. The drumstick is the calf part of the leg, while the thigh is the top part. Drumsticks are inexpensive and delicious, but rarely celebrated. In this recipe, I give the drumstick the recognition it deserves, with a semi-homemade sweet and tangy barbecue sauce. Lather it on and enjoy.*

**DAIRY-FREE, GLUTEN-FREE, NUT-FREE, 5-INGREDIENT, UNDER 30 MINUTES**

**ACCESSORIES:** Grill Grate

2 cups barbecue sauce

Juice of 1 lime

2 tablespoons honey

1 tablespoon hot sauce

Sea salt

Freshly ground black pepper

1 pound chicken drumsticks

1. In a large bowl, combine the barbecue sauce, lime juice, honey, and hot sauce. Season with salt and pepper. Set aside ½ cup of the sauce. Add the drumsticks to the bowl, and toss until evenly coated.

2. Insert the Grill Grate and close the hood. Select GRILL, set the temperature to MEDIUM, and set the time to 20 minutes. Select START/STOP to begin preheating.

3. When the unit beeps to signify it has preheated, place the drumsticks on the Grill Grate. Close the hood and cook for 18 minutes, basting often during cooking.

4. Cooking is complete when the internal temperature of the meat reaches at least 165°F on a food thermometer. If necessary, close the hood and continue cooking for 2 minutes more.

*Per serving: Calories: 433; Total fat: 14g; Saturated fat: 4g; Cholesterol: 95mg; Sodium: 1643mg; Carbohydrates: 55g; Fiber: 1g; Protein: 21g*

# Breaded Chicken Piccata

**SERVES 2 / PREP TIME:** 5 MINUTES / **TOTAL COOK TIME:** 22 MINUTES

*Chicken Piccata is one of my all-time favorite dishes and one of the first dishes I learned to make. It's fairly simple to put together but bursting with flavor. Traditionally, chicken cutlets are served with a sauce of butter, lemon juice, and capers. In this version, the chicken is dredged in flour and air crisped until golden brown. I hope it becomes a favorite in your family, as it has in ours.*

NUT-FREE, UNDER 30 MINUTES, FAMILY FAVORITE

ACCESSORIES: Crisper Basket

2 large eggs

½ cup all-purpose flour

½ teaspoon freshly ground black pepper

2 boneless, skinless chicken breasts

4 tablespoons unsalted butter

Juice of 1 lemon

1 tablespoon capers, drained

1. Insert the Crisper Basket and close the hood. Select AIR CRISP, set the temperature to 375ºF, and set the time to 22 minutes. Select START/STOP to begin preheating.

2. Meanwhile, in a medium shallow bowl, whisk the eggs until they are fully beaten.

3. In a separate medium shallow bowl, combine the flour and black pepper, using a fork to distribute the pepper evenly throughout.

4. Dredge the chicken in the flour to coat it completely, then dip it into the egg, then back in the flour.

5. When the unit beeps to signify it has preheated, place the chicken in the basket. Close the hood and cook for 18 minutes.

6. While the chicken is cooking, melt the butter in a skillet over medium heat. Add the lemon juice and capers, and bring to a simmer. Reduce the heat to low, and simmer for 4 minutes.

CONTINUED ▶

7. After 18 minutes, check the chicken. Cooking is complete when the internal temperature of the meat reaches at least 165°F on a food thermometer. If necessary, close the hood and continue cooking for up to 3 minutes more.

8. Plate the chicken, and drizzle the butter sauce over each serving.

*Per serving: Calories: 522; Total fat: 30g; Saturated fat: 16g; Cholesterol: 290mg; Sodium: 433mg; Carbohydrates: 28g; Fiber: 1g; Protein: 36g*

# Crispy Chicken Cutlets

**SERVES 2 / PREP TIME:** 5 MINUTES / **TOTAL COOK TIME:** 11 MINUTES

*I love crispy chicken cutlets, but I hate shallow-frying the cutlets on the stove. It's cumbersome, it gets messy, and it's a pain to clean up. Luckily, the Ninja® Foodi™ Grill makes quick work of crisping the chicken with just a little bit of oil. Serve with Lemon-Garlic Artichokes (page 48) or top with marinara sauce and mozzarella cheese for a quick and easy chicken Parmesan.*

DAIRY-FREE, NUT-FREE, UNDER 30 MINUTES, FAMILY FAVORITE

ACCESSORIES: Crisper Basket

HACK IT: Make a larger batch and refrigerate whatever you have leftover. When you're ready to eat them again, preheat them in the Crisper Basket at 390°F for 2 to 3 minutes.

- ½ pound boneless, skinless chicken breasts, horizontally sliced in half, into cutlets
- ½ tablespoon extra-virgin olive oil
- ⅛ cup bread crumbs
- ¼ teaspoon sea salt
- ¼ teaspoon freshly ground black pepper
- ¼ teaspoon paprika
- ¼ teaspoon garlic powder
- ⅛ teaspoon onion powder

1. Insert the Crisper Basket and close the hood. Select AIR CRISP, set the temperature to 375°F, and set the time to 11 minutes. Select START/STOP to begin preheating.

2. Brush each side of the chicken cutlets with the oil.

3. Combine the bread crumbs, salt, pepper, paprika, garlic powder, and onion powder in a medium shallow bowl. Dredge the chicken cutlets in the bread crumb mixture, turning several times, to ensure the chicken is fully coated.

4. When the unit beeps to signify it has preheated, place the chicken in the basket. Close the hood and cook for 9 minutes. Cooking is complete when the internal temperature of the meat reaches at least 165°F on a food thermometer. If needed, cook for up to 2 minutes more.

5. Remove the chicken cutlets and serve immediately.

**Per serving:** *Calories: 187; Total fat: 7g; Saturated fat: 1g; Cholesterol: 72mg; Sodium: 341mg; Carbohydrates: 5g; Fiber: 1g; Protein: 25g*

# The Ultimate Turkey Burger

**SERVES 4 / PREP TIME:** 5 MINUTES / **TOTAL COOK TIME:** 13 MINUTES

*What makes this The Ultimate Turkey Burger? Not only does the combination of spices and fresh veggies pack a punch of flavor, but these turkey burger patties turn out char-grilled and juicy every time. There is no complicated technique here, just the Ninja® Foodi™ Grill doing its best work.*

DAIRY-FREE, NUT-FREE, UNDER 30 MINUTES, FAMILY FAVORITE

ACCESSORIES: Grill Grate

VARIATION TIP: Serve your burgers on toasted buns. Add 1 minute to the cook time in step 1, and after removing the burgers from the grill, place the buns on the Grill Grate. Close the hood and cook for the remaining 1 minute.

1 pound ground turkey

½ red onion, minced

1 jalapeño pepper, seeded, stemmed, and minced

3 tablespoons bread crumbs

1½ teaspoons ground cumin

1 teaspoon paprika

½ teaspoon cayenne pepper

½ teaspoon sea salt

½ teaspoon freshly ground black pepper

4 burger buns, for serving

Lettuce, tomato, and cheese, if desired, for serving

Ketchup and mustard, if desired, for serving

1. Insert the Grill Grate and close the hood. Select GRILL, set the temperature to HIGH, and set the time to 13 minutes. Select START/STOP to begin preheating.

2. Meanwhile, in a large bowl, use your hands to combine the ground turkey, red onion, jalapeño pepper, bread crumbs, cumin, paprika, cayenne pepper, salt, and black pepper. Mix until just combined; be careful not to over-work the burger mixture.

3. Dampen your hands with cool water and form the turkey mixture into four patties.

4. When the unit beeps to signify it has preheated, place the burgers on the Grill Grate. Close the hood and cook for 11 minutes.

**5.** After 11 minutes, check the burgers for doneness. Cooking is complete when the internal temperature reaches at least 165°F on a food thermometer. If necessary, close the hood and continue cooking for up to 2 minutes more.

**6.** Once the burgers are done cooking, place each patty on a bun. Top with your preferred fixings, such as lettuce, tomato, cheese, ketchup, and/or mustard.

*Per serving: Calories: 321; Total fat: 12g; Saturated fat: 3g; Cholesterol: 90mg; Sodium: 586mg; Carbohydrates: 27g; Fiber: 2g; Protein: 25g*

Grilled Steak Salad with Blue Cheese Dressing, *page 138*

# Beef, Pork, and Lamb

# Grilled Steak Salad with Blue Cheese Dressing

**SERVES 4 TO 6 / PREP TIME:** 5 MINUTES / **TOTAL COOK TIME:** 16 MINUTES

*Every great steak salad has three main elements: the steak, the dressing, and the fresh vegetables. It's only as good as those three, and in this recipe, all three come together perfectly. Char-grilled steak is piled on top of crisp romaine lettuce, juicy tomatoes, and creamy avocado. A luscious dressing is drizzled over the top to take it to the next level. It's all about crunch and contrast in the quest for the perfect bite.*

NUT-FREE, UNDER
30 MINUTES, FAMILY
FAVORITE

ACCESSORIES: Grill Grate

4 (8-ounce) skirt steaks

Sea salt

Freshly ground
   black pepper

6 cups chopped
   romaine lettuce

¾ cup cherry
   tomatoes, halved

¼ cup blue cheese,
   crumbled

1 cup croutons

2 avocados, peeled
   and sliced

1 cup blue cheese dressing

1. Insert the Grill Grate and close the hood. Select GRILL, set the temperature to HIGH, and set the time to 8 minutes. Select START/STOP to begin preheating.

2. Season the steaks on both sides with the salt and pepper.

3. When the unit beeps to signify it has preheated, place 2 steaks on the Grill Grate. Gently press the steaks down to maximize grill marks. Close the hood and cook for 4 minutes. After 4 minutes, flip the steaks, close the hood, and cook for an additional 4 minutes.

4. Remove the steaks from the grill and transfer to them a cutting board. Tent with aluminum foil.

5. Repeat step 3 with the remaining 2 steaks.

6. While the second set of steaks is cooking, assemble the salad by tossing together the lettuce, tomatoes, blue cheese crumbles, and croutons. Top with the avocado slices.

7. Once the second set of steaks has finished cooking, slice all four of the steaks into thin strips, and place on top of the salad. Drizzle with the blue cheese dressing and serve.

**Per serving:** *Calories: 911; Total fat: 67g; Saturated fat: 18g; Cholesterol: 167mg; Sodium: 1062mg; Carbohydrates: 22g; Fiber: 7g; Protein: 56g*

# Filet Mignon with Pineapple Salsa

**SERVES 4 / PREP TIME:** 15 MINUTES / **TOTAL COOK TIME:** 8 MINUTES

*One of my favorite things about the Ninja® Foodi™ Grill is you can use it to re-create the tastes of summer and the outdoors all year long! Bring the flavors of a resort-style meal into your kitchen at any time with these easy filets. Topped with a sweet, spicy pineapple and jalapeño salsa and ready to eat in less than 30 minutes, this recipe will have you eating in style.*

**DAIRY-FREE, GLUTEN-FREE, NUT-FREE, UNDER 30 MINUTES**

**ACCESSORIES:** Grill Grate

**VARIATION TIP:** There are so many ways to put your own twist on this recipe. Try using other cuts of beef, like flank steak or New York strip, or different salsa variations depending on the season, like fresh mango, pico de gallo, or salsa verde.

- 4 (6- to 8-ounce) filet mignon steaks
- 1 tablespoon canola oil, divided
- Sea salt
- Freshly ground black pepper
- ½ medium pineapple, cored and diced
- 1 medium red onion, diced
- 1 jalapeño pepper, seeded, stemmed, and diced
- 1 tablespoon freshly squeezed lime juice
- ¼ cup chopped fresh cilantro leaves
- Chili powder
- Ground coriander

1. Rub each filet on all sides with ½ tablespoon of the oil, then season with the salt and pepper.

2. Insert the Grill Grate and close the hood. Select GRILL, set temperature to HIGH, and set time to 8 minutes. Select START/STOP to begin preheating.

3. When the unit beeps to signify it has preheated, add the filets to the Grill Grate. Gently press the filets down to maximize grill marks, then close the hood.

4. After 4 minutes, open the hood and flip the filets. Close the hood and continue cooking for an additional 4 minutes, or until the filets' internal temperature reads 125°F on a food thermometer. Remove the filets from the grill; they will continue to cook (called carry-over cooking) to a food-safe temperature even after you've removed them from the grill.

CONTINUED ▶

**5.** Let the filets rest for a total of 10 minutes; this allows the natural juices to redistribute into the steak.

**6.** While the filets rest, in a medium bowl, combine the pineapple, onion, and jalapeño. Stir in the lime juice and cilantro, then season to taste with the chili powder and coriander.

**7.** Plate the filets, and pile the salsa on top of each before serving.

*Per serving: Calories: 571; Total fat: 25g; Saturated fat: 8g; Cholesterol: 192mg; Sodium: 264mg; Carbohydrates: 20g; Fiber: 3g; Protein: 65g*

# Chili-Rubbed Flank Steak

**SERVES 2 / PREP TIME:** 10 MINUTES / **TOTAL COOK TIME:** 8 MINUTES

*Flank steak is quite lean, very flavorful, and best when grilled. This version celebrates the steak with a simple rub. To ensure it's as tender and juicy as possible, serve the steak medium rare and be sure to slice it against the grain. Keep it simple and serve with Blistered Green Beans (page 49) or a hearty dinner salad. You can also thinly slice the steak and make tacos on charred tortillas.*

DAIRY-FREE, GLUTEN-FREE, NUT-FREE, UNDER 30 MINUTES, FAMILY FAVORITE, 5-INGREDIENT

ACCESSORIES: Grill Grate

**1 tablespoon chili powder**

**1 teaspoon dried oregano**

**2 teaspoons ground cumin**

**1 teaspoon sea salt**

**¼ teaspoon freshly ground black pepper**

**2 (8-ounce) flank steaks**

1. Insert the Grill Grate and close the hood. Select GRILL, set the temperature to HIGH, and set the time to 8 minutes. Select START/STOP to begin preheating.

2. In a small bowl, mix together the chili powder, oregano, cumin, salt, and pepper. Use your hands to rub the spice mixture on all sides of the steaks.

3. When the unit beeps to signify it has preheated, place the steaks on the Grill Grate. Gently press the steaks down to maximize grill marks. Close the hood and cook for 4 minutes. After 4 minutes, flip the steaks, close the hood, and cook for 4 minutes more.

4. Remove the steaks from the grill, and transfer them to a cutting board. Let rest for 5 minutes before slicing and serving.

*Per serving: Calories: 363; Total fat: 15g; Saturated fat: 6g; Cholesterol: 100mg; Sodium: 1008mg; Carbohydrates: 4g; Fiber: 2g; Protein: 51g*

# Soy and Garlic Steak Kebabs

**SERVES 4 / PREP TIME:** 5 MINUTES, PLUS 30 MINUTES TO MARINATE
**TOTAL COOK TIME:** 12 MINUTES

*These kebabs are as simple as they are delicious. I love the combination of tender beef and charred vegetables in this recipe, but it is the marinade that truly sets this recipe apart. A generous amount of marinade and a little time ensure that every bite is bursting with the rich flavors of soy sauce, garlic, ginger, and sesame oil. Not to mention a little extra time in the marinade means super tender beef. Prepare your marinade and steak the day before—you can even refrigerate the steak in the marinade overnight.*

**DAIRY-FREE, NUT-FREE, FAMILY FAVORITE**

**ACCESSORIES:** Grill Grate and Ninja® Foodi™ Grill Kebab Skewers (or wood skewers)

**SUBSTITUTION TIP:** While you can swap the steak for chicken or shrimp, I recommend sticking with New York strip or top sirloin. These cuts have great flavor and are very tender when marinated and grilled.

¾ **cup soy sauce**

5 **garlic cloves, minced**

3 **tablespoons sesame oil**

½ **cup canola oil**

⅓ **cup sugar**

¼ **teaspoon dried ground ginger**

2 **(10- to 12-ounce) New York strip steaks, cut in 2-inch cubes**

1 **cup whole white mushrooms**

1 **red bell pepper, seeded, and cut into 2-inch cubes**

1 **red onion, cut into 2-inch wedges**

1. In a medium bowl, whisk together the soy sauce, garlic, sesame oil, canola oil, sugar, and ginger until well combined. Add the steak and toss to coat. Cover and refrigerate for at least 30 minutes.

2. Insert the Grill Grate and close the hood. Select GRILL, set the temperature to MEDIUM, and set the time to 12 minutes. Select START/STOP to begin preheating.

3. While the unit is preheating, assemble the skewers in the following order: steak, mushroom, bell pepper, onion. Ensure the ingredients are pushed almost completely down to the end of the skewers.

CONTINUED ▶

## Soy and Garlic Steak Kebabs continued

**4.** When the unit beeps to signify it has preheated, place the skewers on the Grill Grate. Close the hood and cook for 8 minutes without flipping.

**5.** After 8 minutes, check the steak for desired doneness, cooking up to 4 minutes more if desired.

**6.** When cooking is complete, serve immediately.

Per serving: *Calories: 647; Total fat: 45g; Saturated fat: 12g; Cholesterol: 135mg; Sodium: 1001mg; Carbohydrates: 17g; Fiber: 1g; Protein: 47g*

# Beef Bulgogi

**SERVES 4 / PREP TIME:** 5 MINUTES, PLUS 1 HOUR TO MARINATE
**TOTAL COOK TIME:** 5 MINUTES

*The first time I made this recipe was for an international summit at Ninja®. I wanted to show folks from all over the world how the Ninja Foodi™ Grill could be applied to traditional regional recipes. In this recipe, char-grilled marinated beef results in a sweet and smoky Korean classic.*

**DAIRY-FREE, NUT-FREE**

**ACCESSORIES:** Grill Grate, Crisper Basket

**HACK IT:** To make the steak easier to slice, stick it in the freezer for an hour before you cut it and put it in the marinade.

⅓ cup soy sauce

2 tablespoons sesame oil

2½ tablespoons brown sugar

3 garlic cloves, minced

½ teaspoon freshly ground black pepper

1 pound rib eye steak, thinly sliced

2 scallions, thinly sliced, for garnish

Toasted sesame seeds, for garnish

1. In a small bowl, whisk together the soy sauce, sesame oil, brown sugar, garlic, and black pepper until fully combined.

2. Place the beef into a large shallow bowl, and pour the sauce over the slices. Cover and refrigerate for 1 hour.

3. Insert the Grill Grate and close the hood. Select GRILL, set the temperature to MEDIUM, and set the time to 5 minutes. Select START/STOP to begin preheating.

4. When the unit beeps to signify it has preheated, place the beef onto the Grill Grate. Close the hood and cook for 4 minutes without flipping.

5. After 4 minutes, check the steak for desired doneness, cooking for up to 1 minute more, if desired.

6. When cooking is complete, top with scallions and sesame seeds and serve immediately.

*Per serving: Calories: 403; Total fat: 31g; Saturated fat: 13g; Cholesterol: 76mg; Sodium: 1263mg; Carbohydrates: 8g; Fiber: 0g; Protein: 22g*

# Meatball Sandwiches with Mozzarella and Basil

**SERVES 4 / PREP TIME:** 5 MINUTES / **TOTAL COOK TIME:** 10 MINUTES

*We always keep a few staples in the freezer, so we can make quick and easy meals. I'm talking cauliflower gnocchi, meatballs, and, of course, frozen fruits and vegetables. This recipe is a family favorite because it's only five ingredients and takes about 15 minutes from freezer to table. You can also use the Air Crisp function to reheat leftover meatballs instead of using frozen, if you prefer.*

NUT-FREE, UNDER 30 MINUTES, FAMILY FAVORITE, 5-INGREDIENT

**ACCESSORIES:** Crisper Basket

**DID YOU KNOW?** When air-crisping, shaking or flipping your food halfway through cooking is a must to ensure your food is evenly crisped on all sides. The more you shake, the more evenly your food will cook.

**12 frozen meatballs**

**8 slices mozzarella cheese**

**4 sub rolls, halved lengthwise**

**½ cup marinara sauce, warmed**

**12 fresh basil leaves**

1. Insert the Crisper Basket and close the hood. Select AIR CRISP, set the temperature to 350ºF, and set the time to 10 minutes. Select START/STOP to begin preheating.

2. When the unit beeps to signify it has preheated, place the meatballs in the basket. Close the hood and cook for 5 minutes.

3. After 5 minutes, shake the basket of meatballs. Place the basket back in the unit and close the hood to resume cooking.

4. While the meatballs are cooking, place two slices of mozzarella cheese on each sub roll. Use a spoon to spread the marinara sauce on top of the cheese slices. Press three leaves of basil into the sauce on each roll.

5. When cooking is complete, place three meatballs on each sub roll. Serve immediately.

*Per serving: Calories: 537; Total fat: 27g; Saturated fat: 13g; Cholesterol: 80mg; Sodium: 1243mg; Carbohydrates: 46g; Fiber: 4g; Protein: 34g*

# Gochujang-Marinated Baby Back Ribs

**SERVES 4 / PREP TIME:** 10 MINUTES, PLUS 6 HOURS TO MARINATE
**TOTAL COOK TIME:** 22 MINUTES

*Sticky. Spicy. Salty. Sweet. These Gochujang-Marinated Baby Back Ribs are seriously addictive. If you haven't used gochujang yet, I can't wait for you to try it. This not-so-secret Korean ingredient adds a kick and depth of flavor to just about everything.*

**DAIRY-FREE, NUT-FREE**

**ACCESSORIES:** Grill Grate

**SUBSTITUTION TIP:**
Don't have orange juice? Try swapping in another citrusy juice here, like lime or lemon.

- ¼ cup gochujang paste
- ¼ cup soy sauce
- ¼ cup freshly squeezed orange juice
- 2 tablespoons apple cider vinegar
- 2 tablespoons sesame oil
- 6 garlic cloves, minced
- 1½ tablespoons brown sugar
- 1 tablespoon grated fresh ginger
- 1 teaspoon salt
- 4 (8- to 10-ounce) baby back ribs

1. In a medium bowl, add the gochujang paste, soy sauce, orange juice, vinegar, oil, garlic, sugar, ginger, and salt, and stir to combine.

2. Place the baby back ribs on a baking sheet and coat all sides with the sauce. Cover with aluminum foil and refrigerate for 6 hours.

3. Insert the Grill Grate and close the hood. Select GRILL, set the temperature to MEDIUM, and set the time to 22 minutes. Select START/STOP to begin preheating.

4. When the unit beeps to signify it has preheated, place the ribs on the Grill Grate. Close the hood and cook for 11 minutes. After 11 minutes, flip the ribs, close the hood, and cook for an additional 11 minutes.

5. When cooking is complete, serve immediately.

*Per serving: Calories: 826; Total fat: 64g; Saturated fat: 22g; Cholesterol: 191mg; Sodium: 2113mg; Carbohydrates: 19g; Fiber: 1g; Protein: 41g*

# Bourbon Barbecue– Glazed Pork Chops

**SERVES 4 / PREP TIME:** 5 MINUTES / **TOTAL COOK TIME:** 35 MINUTES

*These are not your mother's pork chops. Juicy, smoky, and delicious, these pork chops are grilled to perfection. Not to mention, bourbon and barbecue go hand in hand. The subtle smokiness of bourbon perfectly complements the smokiness of char-grilled pork. No tough, dried-out pork chops here. The glaze adds flavor and keeps the lean protein from drying out.*

DAIRY-FREE, NUT-FREE, FAMILY FAVORITE

ACCESSORIES: Grill Grate

HACK IT: You can make the barbecue sauce in advance and store in the refrigerator in an airtight container for up to 5 days.

2 cups ketchup

¾ cup bourbon

¼ cup apple cider vinegar

¼ cup soy sauce

1 cup packed brown sugar

3 tablespoons Worcestershire sauce

½ tablespoon dry mustard powder

4 boneless pork chops

Sea salt

Freshly ground black pepper

1. In a medium saucepan over high heat, combine the ketchup, bourbon, vinegar, soy sauce, sugar, Worcestershire sauce, and mustard powder. Stir to combine and bring to a boil.

2. Reduce the heat to low and simmer, uncovered and stirring occasionally, for 20 minutes. The barbecue sauce will thicken while cooking. Once thickened, remove the pan from the heat and set aside.

3. While the barbecue sauce is cooking, insert the Grill Grate into the unit and close the hood. Select GRILL, set the temperature to MEDIUM, and set the time to 15 minutes. Select START/STOP to begin preheating.

CONTINUED ▶

4. When the unit beeps to signify it has preheated, place the pork chops on the Grill Grate. Close the hood, and cook for 8 minutes. After 8 minutes, flip the pork chops and baste the cooked side with the barbecue sauce. Close the hood, and cook for 5 minutes more.

5. Open the hood, and flip the pork chops again, basting both sides with the barbecue sauce. Close the hood, and cook for the final 2 minutes.

6. When cooking is complete, season with salt and pepper and serve immediately.

*Per serving: Calories: 361; Total fat: 14g; Saturated fat: 5g; Cholesterol: 55mg; Sodium: 1412mg; Carbohydrates: 26g; Fiber: 0g; Protein: 26g*

# Honey-Glazed Pork Tenderloin

**SERVES 4 / PREP TIME:** 5 MINUTES / **TOTAL COOK TIME:** 15 TO 20 MINUTES

*When grilling, a marinade or glaze can infuse flavor into the meat, so it's moist and flavorful. Here, just a few simple ingredients from the pantry create a delicious, sweet glaze for the perfect pork tenderloin. The high heat of the grill transforms the marinade into a gorgeous caramelized crust while keeping the pork juicy on the inside.*

**DAIRY-FREE, NUT-FREE, UNDER 30 MINUTES, FAMILY FAVORITE, 5-INGREDIENT**

**ACCESSORIES:** Grill Grate

2 tablespoons honey

1 tablespoon soy sauce

½ teaspoon garlic powder

½ teaspoon sea salt

1 (1½-pound) pork tenderloin

1. Insert the Grill Grate and close the hood. Select GRILL, set the temperature to MEDIUM, and set the time to 20 minutes. Select START/STOP to begin preheating.

2. Meanwhile, in a small bowl, combine the honey, soy sauce, garlic powder, and salt.

3. When the unit beeps to signify it has preheated, place the pork tenderloin on the Grill Grate. Baste all sides with the honey glaze. Close the hood and cook for 8 minutes. After 8 minutes, flip the pork tenderloin and baste with any remaining glaze. Close the hood and cook for 7 minutes more.

4. Cooking is complete when the internal temperature of the pork reaches 145°F on a food thermometer. If needed, cook for up to 5 minutes more.

5. Remove the pork, and set it on a cutting board to rest for 5 minutes. Slice and serve.

*Per serving: Calories: 215; Total fat: 6g; Saturated fat: 2g; Cholesterol: 98mg; Sodium: 558mg; Carbohydrates: 9g; Fiber: 0g; Protein: 30g*

# Charred Korean-Style Steak Tips

**SERVES 4 / PREP TIME:** 5 MINUTES, PLUS 30 MINUTES TO MARINATE
**TOTAL COOK TIME:** 13 MINUTES

*This recipe was inspired by the pre-marinated steak tips I often pick up at the market down the street. With this version, the beef is marinated with brown sugar, soy sauce, garlic, and a few other pantry staples.*

**DAIRY-FREE, NUT-FREE**

**ACCESSORIES:** Grill Grate

**VARIATION TIP:** This marinade works perfectly on flank steak if you can't find beef tips. Cut the flank steak into cubes before marinating, and follow the same cook time and temperature.

**4 garlic cloves, minced**

**½ apple, peeled and grated**

**3 tablespoons sesame oil**

**3 tablespoons brown sugar**

**⅓ cup soy sauce**

**1 teaspoon freshly ground black pepper**

**Sea salt**

**1½ pounds beef tips**

1. In a medium bowl, combine the garlic, apple, sesame oil, sugar, soy sauce, pepper, and salt until well mixed.

2. Place the beef tips in a large shallow bowl and pour the marinade over them. Cover and refrigerate for 30 minutes.

3. Insert the Grill Grate and close the hood. Select GRILL, set the temperature to MEDIUM, and set the time to 13 minutes. Select START/STOP to begin preheating.

4. When the unit beeps to signify it has preheated, place the steak tips on the Grill Grate. Close the hood and cook for 11 minutes.

5. Cooking is complete to medium doneness when the internal temperature of the meat reaches 145°F on a food thermometer. If desired, cook for up to 2 minutes more.

6. Remove the steak, and set it on a cutting board to rest for 5 minutes. Serve.

*Per serving: Calories: 507; Total fat: 34g; Saturated fat: 11g; Cholesterol: 128mg; Sodium: 1295mg; Carbohydrates: 13g; Fiber: 1g; Protein: 35g*

# Jalapeño Popper Burgers

**SERVES 4 / PREP TIME:** 5 MINUTES / **TOTAL COOK TIME:** 9 MINUTES

*If there is one recipe you have to know how to make on a grill, it's a burger. But this isn't just any burger. This is your favorite game day appetizer reimagined. Stuffed with jalapeño peppers, Cheddar cheese, and bacon, then seasoned to perfection, these are burgers done right. Serve them on toasted buns with melted pepper Jack cheese and all the fixings.*

NUT-FREE, UNDER
30 MINUTES, FAMILY
FAVORITE

ACCESSORIES: Grill Grate,
Crisper Basket

VARIATION TIP: Looking
to take the flavor of
your burgers to the next
level? Slice and seed
the jalapeño peppers,
and blister them in the
Foodi™ Grill on MAX
temperature for 3 to
5 minutes before mincing
them for your filling.

2 jalapeño peppers,
  seeded, stemmed,
  and minced

½ cup shredded
  Cheddar cheese

4 ounces cream cheese,
  at room temperature

4 slices bacon, cooked
  and crumbled

2 pounds ground beef

½ teaspoon chili powder

¼ teaspoon paprika

¼ teaspoon freshly
  ground black pepper

4 hamburger buns

4 slices pepper Jack cheese

Lettuce, sliced tomato,
  and sliced red onion,
  for topping (optional)

1. Insert the Grill Grate and close the hood. Select GRILL, set the temperature to HIGH, and set the time to 9 minutes. Select START/STOP to begin preheating.

2. In a medium bowl, combine the peppers, Cheddar cheese, cream cheese, and bacon until well combined.

3. Form the ground beef into 8 ¼-inch-thick patties. Spoon some of the filling mixture onto four of the patties, then place a second patty on top of each to make four burgers. Use your fingers to pinch the edges of the patties together to seal in the filling. Reshape the patties with your hands as needed.

**4.** Combine the chili powder, paprika, and pepper in a small bowl. Sprinkle the mixture onto both sides of the burgers.

**5.** When the units beeps to signify it has preheated, place the burgers on the Grill Grate. Close the hood and cook for 4 minutes without flipping. Cooking is complete when the internal temperature of the beef reaches at least 145ºF on a food thermometer. If needed, cook for up to 5 more minutes.

**6.** Place the burgers on the hamburger buns and top with pepper Jack cheese. Add lettuce, tomato, and red onion, if desired.

*Per serving: Calories: 803; Total fat: 49g; Saturated fat: 23g; Cholesterol: 227mg; Sodium: 1364mg; Carbohydrates: 24g; Fiber: 1g; Protein: 67g*

# Rosemary Rack of Lamb Chops

**SERVES 2 / PREP TIME:** 5 MINUTES, PLUS 2 HOURS TO MARINATE
**TOTAL COOK TIME:** 14 MINUTES

*The surprising thing about rack of lamb is that it's super easy to make. While often viewed as an elegant dish for a special occasions—and it is—it actually comes together with little prep and a quick cook time. Just make sure you have some time to let it marinate, so the juicy, tender lamb is bursting with rosemary and garlic in each and every bite.*

DAIRY-FREE, GLUTEN-FREE, NUT-FREE, 5-INGREDIENT

ACCESSORIES: Grill Grate, Crisper Basket

HACK IT: Have some room left on your Grill Grate? Add some vegetables lightly coated in canola oil to complete your meal. Zucchini or squash will cook in a similar time, and you can flip them when you flip the lamb.

**3 tablespoons extra-virgin olive oil**

**1 garlic clove, minced**

**1 tablespoon fresh rosemary, chopped**

**½ rack lamb (4 bones)**

**Sea salt**

**Freshly ground black pepper**

**1.** Combine the oil, garlic, and rosemary in a large bowl. Season the rack of lamb with the salt and pepper, then place the lamb in the bowl, using tongs to turn and coat fully in the oil mixture. Cover and refrigerate for 2 hours.

**2.** Insert the Grill Grate and close the hood. Select GRILL, set the temperature to HIGH, and set the time to 14 minutes. Select START/STOP to begin preheating.

**3.** When the unit beeps to signify it has preheated, place the lamb on the Grill Grate. Close the hood and cook for 6 minutes. After 6 minutes, flip the lamb and continue cooking for 6 minutes more.

**4.** Cooking is complete when the internal temperature of the lamb reaches 145°F on a food thermometer. If needed, cook for up to 2 minutes more.

*Per serving: Calories: 378; Total fat: 31g; Saturated fat: 7g; Cholesterol: 75mg; Sodium: 315mg; Carbohydrates: 1g; Fiber: 1g; Protein: 23g*

**Rum-Soaked Grilled Pineapple Sundaes,** *page 162*

# Desserts

# Rum-Soaked Grilled Pineapple Sundaes

**SERVES 6** / **PREP TIME:** 15 MINUTES / **TOTAL COOK TIME:** 8 MINUTES

*Fresh pineapple and rum are a quintessential tropical pairing. Here, the bright, fresh pineapple is coated in a rum and sugar glaze that caramelizes on the grill. It's then turned into a sundae with a scoop of vanilla ice cream. If you really want to channel the tropics, add a sprinkle of toasted coconut flakes for a piña colada twist. Just looking for a sweet snack by the pool? Dice the pineapple after grilling, serve with toothpicks, and skip the ice cream.*

GLUTEN-FREE, NUT-FREE, VEGETARIAN, UNDER 30 MINUTES, FAMILY FAVORITE, 5-INGREDIENT

ACCESSORIES: Grill Grate

**DID YOU KNOW?** You can make a quick and easy rum sauce topping by reducing the strained sauce in a small saucepan over medium-high heat. Bring the sauce to a simmer, then reduce the heat to medium-low and simmer for 6 to 8 minutes.

½ **cup dark rum**

½ **cup packed brown sugar**

1 **teaspoon ground cinnamon, plus more for garnish**

1 **pineapple, cored and sliced**

**Vanilla ice cream, for serving**

1. In a large shallow bowl or storage container, combine the rum, sugar, and cinnamon. Add the pineapple slices and arrange them in a single layer. Coat with the mixture, then let soak for at least 5 minutes per side.

2. Insert the Grill Grate and close the hood. Select GRILL, set the temperature to MAX, and set the time to 8 minutes. Select START/STOP to begin preheating.

3. While the unit is preheating, strain the extra rum sauce from the pineapple.

4. When the unit beeps to signify it has preheated, place the fruit on the Grill Grate in a single layer (you may need to do this in multiple batches). Gently press the fruit down to maximize grill marks. Close the hood and grill for about 6 to 8 minutes without flipping. If working in batches, remove the pineapple, and repeat this step for the remaining pineapple slices.

**5.** When cooking is complete, remove, and top each pineapple ring with a scoop of ice cream. Sprinkle with cinnamon and serve immediately.

*Per serving:* *Calories: 240; Total fat: 4g; Saturated fat: 2g; Cholesterol: 15mg; Sodium: 32mg; Carbohydrates: 43g; Fiber: 3g; Protein: 2g*

# Charred Peaches with Bourbon Butter Sauce

SERVES 4 / PREP TIME: 10 MINUTES / TOTAL COOK TIME: 12 MINUTES

*In the summer when peaches are at their peak, stock up and make these Charred Peaches with Bourbon Butter Sauce. After all, the combination of sweet peaches and spicy bourbon scream summer in the American South. To get the best char on the peaches, refrain from moving them around on the grill and let the Ninja® Foodi™ Grill create a smoky char. Then drizzle the luscious bourbon sauce over the peaches and top with vanilla ice cream, if desired.*

GLUTEN-FREE, VEGETARIAN, UNDER 30 MINUTES, 5-INGREDIENT

ACCESSORIES: Grill Grate

**DID YOU KNOW?** Brown butter, also known as *buerre noisette*, occurs when you melt butter over medium heat for a period of time. First, the butter melts, then it foams and turns a blond color. Finally, after about 5 minutes, the milk solids toast and turn brown.

**4 tablespoons salted butter**

**¼ cup bourbon**

**½ cup brown sugar**

**4 ripe peaches, halved and pitted**

**¼ cup candied pecans**

1. Insert the Grill Grate and close the hood. Select GRILL, set the temperature to MAX, and set the time to 12 minutes. Select START/STOP to begin preheating.

2. While the unit is preheating, in a saucepan over medium heat, melt the butter for about 5 minutes. Once the butter is browned, remove the pan from the heat and carefully add the bourbon.

3. Return the saucepan to medium-high heat and add the brown sugar. Bring to a boil and let the sugar dissolve for 5 minutes, stirring occasionally.

4. Pour the bourbon butter sauce into a medium shallow bowl and arrange the peaches cut-side down to coat in the sauce.

**5.** When the unit beeps to signify it has preheated, place the fruit on the Grill Grate in a single layer (you may need to do this in multiple batches). Gently press the fruit down to maximize grill marks. Close the hood and grill for 10 to 12 minutes without flipping. If working in batches, repeat this step for all the peaches.

**6.** When cooking is complete, remove the peaches and top each with the pecans. Drizzle with the remaining bourbon butter sauce and serve immediately.

**Per serving:** *Calories: 309; Total fat: 16g; Saturated fat: 8g; Cholesterol: 31mg; Sodium: 106mg; Carbohydrates: 34g; Fiber: 4g; Protein: 2g*

# Grilled Pound Cake with Fresh Mint and Berries

**SERVES 6 / PREP TIME:** 10 MINUTES / **TOTAL COOK TIME:** 8 MINUTES

*This is an excellent example of a semi-homemade dessert. When you're short on time, pick up a pound cake and fresh berries. With a few simple tricks, you can transform these ingredients into a delicious and decadent dessert. A few minutes on the grill revamps a slice of store-bought pound cake, and a little sugar and mint transforms fresh berries into a super sweet treat. Together, the pound cake and berries are a unique twist on strawberry shortcake. You can even add a dollop of whipped cream.*

NUT-FREE, VEGETARIAN, UNDER 30 MINUTES

ACCESSORIES: Grill Grate

VARIATION TIP: If you prefer a fruit compote to fresh berries, simply bring the berries and sugar to a boil on the stove with a splash of water and lemon juice, then lower the heat and let the mixture reduce while it simmers.

3 tablespoons unsalted butter, at room temperature

6 slices pound cake, sliced about 1-inch thick

1 cup fresh raspberries

1 cup fresh blueberries

3 tablespoons sugar

½ tablespoon fresh mint, minced

1. Insert the Grill Grate and close the hood. Select GRILL, set the temperature to MAX, and set the time to 8 minutes. Select START/STOP to begin preheating.

2. While the unit is preheating, evenly spread the butter on both sides of each slice of pound cake.

3. When the unit beeps to signify it has preheated, place the pound cake on the Grill Grate. Close the hood and cook for 2 minutes.

4. After 2 minutes, flip the pound cake and cook for 2 minutes more, until golden brown. Repeat steps 3 and 4 for all of the pound cake slices.

**5.** While the pound cake cooks, in a medium mixing bowl, combine the raspberries, blueberries, sugar, and mint.

**6.** When cooking is complete, plate the cake slices and serve topped with the berry mixture.

*Per serving: Calories: 215; Total fat: 12g; Saturated fat: 7g; Cholesterol: 82mg; Sodium: 161mg; Carbohydrates: 27g; Fiber: 2g; Protein: 2g*

# Chocolate-Hazelnut and Strawberry Grilled Dessert Pizza

**SERVES 4 / PREP TIME:** 10 MINUTES / **TOTAL COOK TIME:** 6 MINUTES

*Pizza dough can be used in so many ways, from a char-grilled pizza to zesty garlic knots—and even dessert. This recipe follows the same principles for cooking pizza on the grill as my Grilled Pizza with Eggs and Greens (page 33) and Veggie Lovers' Grilled Pizza (page 70), but instead of topping the pizza with cheese, simply add chocolate-hazelnut spread and fresh fruit. Who says you can't have pizza for every meal of the day?*

DAIRY-FREE, VEGETARIAN, UNDER 30 MINUTES, FAMILY FAVORITE, 5-INGREDIENT

ACCESSORIES: Grill Grate

VARIATION TIP: Make this dessert pizza your own by swapping out the strawberries for whatever fruit or berries are in season. You can also use fresh or grilled banana. Want to make this dessert even more decadent? Add a few dollops of mascarpone.

2 tablespoons all-purpose flour, plus more as needed

½ store-bought pizza dough (about 8 ounces)

1 tablespoon canola oil

1 cup sliced fresh strawberries

1 tablespoon sugar

½ cup chocolate-hazelnut spread

1. Insert the Grill Grate and close the hood. Select GRILL, set the temperature to MAX, and set the time to 6 minutes. Select START/STOP to begin preheating.

2. While the unit is preheating, dust a clean work surface with the flour. Place the dough on the floured surface, and roll it out to a 9-inch round of even thickness. Dust your rolling pin and work surface with additional flour, as needed, to ensure the dough does not stick.

3. Brush the surface of the rolled-out dough evenly with half the oil. Flip the dough over, and brush with the remaining oil. Poke the dough with a fork 5 or 6 times across its surface to prevent air pockets from forming during cooking.

4. When the unit beeps to signify it has preheated, place the dough on the Grill Grate. Close the hood and cook for 3 minutes.

CONTINUED ▶

## Chocolate-Hazelnut and Strawberry Grilled Dessert Pizza continued

5. After 3 minutes, flip the dough. Close the hood and continue cooking for the remaining 3 minutes.

6. Meanwhile, in a medium mixing bowl, combine the strawberries and sugar.

7. Transfer the pizza to a cutting board and let cool. Top with the chocolate-hazelnut spread and strawberries. Cut into pieces and serve.

*Per serving: Calories: 377; Total fat: 18g; Saturated fat: 4g; Cholesterol: 0mg; Sodium: 258mg; Carbohydrates: 53g; Fiber: 4g; Protein: 7g*

# Blueberry Cobbler

**SERVES 6 / PREP TIME:** 15 MINUTES / **TOTAL COOK TIME:** 30 MINUTES

*Cobblers are one of my favorite desserts because they're so easy to customize based on what's in season. I love blueberries in the peak of summer, but peaches, apples, strawberries, and rhubarb make excellent cobblers, too. You can also put your own twist on this recipe by combining different fillings. Try blueberry and strawberry for your next Fourth of July barbecue, or apple and pecans in the fall.*

**NUT-FREE, VEGETARIAN, FAMILY FAVORITE**

**ACCESSORIES:** Ninja® Multi-Purpose Pan or 8-inch baking pan

**VARIATION TIP:** If fruit is not at its peak, swap out fresh for frozen. Just let the fruit thaw slightly before cooking.

4 cups fresh blueberries

1 teaspoon grated lemon zest

1 cup sugar, plus 2 tablespoons

1 cup all-purpose flour, plus 2 tablespoons

Juice of 1 lemon

2 teaspoons baking powder

¼ teaspoon salt

6 tablespoons unsalted butter

¾ cup whole milk

⅛ teaspoon ground cinnamon

1. In a medium bowl, combine the blueberries, lemon zest, 2 tablespoons of sugar, 2 tablespoons of flour, and lemon juice.

2. In a medium bowl, combine the remaining 1 cup of flour and 1 cup of sugar, baking powder, and salt. Cut the butter into the flour mixture until it forms an even crumb texture. Stir in the milk until a dough forms.

3. Select BAKE, set the temperature to 350°F, and set the time to 30 minutes. Select START/STOP to begin preheating.

4. Meanwhile, pour the blueberry mixture into the Multi-Purpose Pan, spreading it evenly across the pan. Gently pour the batter over the blueberry mixture, then sprinkle the cinnamon over the top.

CONTINUED ▶

## Blueberry Cobbler continued

5. When the unit beeps to signify it has preheated, place the pan directly in the pot. Close the hood and cook for 30 minutes, until lightly golden.

6. When cooking is complete, serve warm.

*Per serving:* *Calories: 408; Total fat: 13g; Saturated fat: 8g; Cholesterol: 34mg; Sodium: 194mg; Carbohydrates: 72g; Fiber: 3g; Protein: 5g*

# Peanut Butter and Marshmallow Banana Boats

**SERVES 4 / PREP TIME:** 10 MINUTES / **TOTAL COOK TIME:** 6 MINUTES

*Banana boats are a campfire favorite for my family every summer. A twist on a traditional s'more, this version uses a banana as the base and is simple to assemble and customize with everyone's favorite toppings. Simply split a banana in the peel, stuff to your heart's content with your favorite sweets, then place in the Ninja® Foodi™ Grill. In minutes, the heat transforms it into a delicious concoction that can only be eaten with a spoon and a big smile on your face.*

DAIRY-FREE,
VEGETARIAN,
UNDER 30 MINUTES,
5-INGREDIENT, FAMILY
FAVORITE

**ACCESSORIES:** Grill Grate

**VARIATION TIP:** While I chose my three favorite s'more toppings, have fun with different combinations. Try the classic s'more combo of marshmallow, chocolate, and graham cracker, or mix it up with berries and nuts.

**4 ripe bananas**

**1 cup mini marshmallows**

**½ cup chocolate chips**

**½ cup peanut butter chips**

1. Insert the Grill Grate and close the hood. Select GRILL, set the temperature to MEDIUM, and set the time to 6 minutes. Select START/STOP to begin preheating.

2. While the unit is preheating, slice each banana lengthwise while still in its peel, making sure not to cut all the way through. Using both hands, pull the banana peel open like you would a book, revealing the banana inside. Divide the marshmallows, chocolate chips, and peanut butter chips among the bananas, stuffing them inside the skin.

3. When the unit beeps to signify it has preheated, place the stuffed banana on the Grill Grate. Close the hood and cook for 4 to 6 minutes, until the chocolate is melted and the marshmallows are toasted.

*Per serving: Calories: 505; Total fat: 18g; Saturated fat: 13g; Cholesterol: 12mg; Sodium: 103mg; Carbohydrates: 82g; Fiber: 6g; Protein: 10g*

# Churros with Chocolate Sauce

**SERVES 8 / PREP TIME:** 15 MINUTES, PLUS 1 HOUR TO REST
**TOTAL COOK TIME:** 30 MINUTES

*I'll never forget the first time I made churros. I was in sixth grade, and my friend and I did a project on Spain. We made churros to accompany the report. I fell in love with the fried dough pastry immediately. They're crispy on the outside, soft and tender on the inside, and they have a cinnamon-sugar crust that no one can resist. In this recipe, the Ninja® Foodi™ Grill gives you the classic churro crunch you love, without a ton of oil and the need for a deep fryer.*

**NUT-FREE, VEGETARIAN, FAMILY FAVORITE**

**ACCESSORIES:** Crisper Basket

**HACK IT:** The trickiest part of this recipe is getting the batter into the air fryer. If piping the strips gets tricky, chill the batter between batches or skip the sticks altogether and make round, donut-hole shapes instead.

1 cup water

1 stick unsalted butter, cut into 8 pieces

½ cup sugar, plus 1 tablespoon

1 cup all-purpose flour

1 teaspoon vanilla extract

3 large eggs

2 teaspoons ground cinnamon

Nonstick cooking spray

4 ounces dark chocolate, chopped

¼ cup Greek yogurt

**1.** In a medium saucepan over medium-high heat, combine the water, butter, and the 1 tablespoon of sugar. Bring to a simmer. Add the flour, stirring it in quickly. Continue to cook, stirring constantly, until the mixture is thick, about 3 minutes. Transfer to a large bowl.

**2.** Using a spoon, beat the flour mixture for about 1 minute, until cooled slightly. Stir in the vanilla, then the eggs, one at a time.

**3.** Transfer the dough to a plastic bag or a piping bag. Let the dough rest for 1 hour at room temperature.

**4.** Insert the Crisper Basket and close the hood. Select AIR CRISP, set the temperature to 375°F, and set the time to 30 minutes. Select START/STOP to begin preheating.

**5.** Meanwhile, in a medium shallow bowl, combine the cinnamon and remaining ½ cup of sugar.

CONTINUED ▶

6. When the unit beeps to signify it has preheated, spray the basket with the nonstick cooking spray. Take the plastic bag with your dough and cut off one corner. Pipe the batter directly into the Crisper Basket, making 6 (3-inch-long) churros, placed at least ½ inch apart. Close the hood and cook for 10 minutes.

7. Meanwhile, in a small microwave-safe mixing bowl, melt the chocolate in the microwave, stirring it after every 30 seconds, until completely melted and smooth. Add the yogurt and whisk until smooth.

8. After 10 minutes, carefully transfer the churros to the sugar mixture and toss to coat evenly. Repeat piping and air crisping with the remaining batter, adding time as needed.

9. Serve the churros with the warm chocolate dipping sauce.

*Per serving: Calories: 313; Total fat: 18g; Saturated fat: 11g; Cholesterol: 95mg; Sodium: 118mg; Carbohydrates: 34g; Fiber: 1g; Protein: 6g*

# Glazed Cinnamon Biscuit Bites

**SERVES 8 / PREP TIME:** 15 MINUTES / **TOTAL COOK TIME:** 12 MINUTES

*A cross between your favorite biscuits and glazed donuts, these little bites are easy, delicious, and so much fun. They are perfect for a sweet breakfast treat, an afternoon snack, or a bite-size dessert. Make this recipe your own by jazzing up the glaze. Swap lemon juice for water, or forget the glaze and dip the cooked bites in cinnamon sugar instead.*

NUT-FREE, VEGETARIAN, UNDER 30 MINUTES, FAMILY FAVORITE

**ACCESSORIES:** Crisper Basket

**HACK IT:** It's important to keep the small pieces of butter cold to ensure flaky biscuits. I like to freeze the butter in advance, then grate it to ensure tiny, cold pieces are incorporated into the dough.

⅔ **cup all-purpose flour, plus additional for dusting**

⅔ **cup whole-wheat flour**

2 **tablespoons granulated sugar**

1 **teaspoon baking powder**

¼ **teaspoon ground cinnamon**

¼ **teaspoon sea salt**

4 **tablespoons salted butter, cold and cut into small pieces**

⅓ **cup whole milk**

**Nonstick cooking spray**

2 **cups powdered sugar**

3 **tablespoons water**

1. In a large bowl, combine the all-purpose flour, whole-wheat flour, sugar, baking powder, cinnamon, and salt. Add the cold butter pieces, and cut them into the flour mixture using a pastry cutter or a fork, until well-combined and the mixture resembles a course meal. Add the milk to the mixture, and stir together until the dough comes together into a ball.

2. Insert the Crisper Basket and close the hood. Select AIR CRISP, set the temperature to 350°F, and set the time to 12 minutes. Select START/STOP to begin preheating.

3. While the unit is preheating, dust a clean work surface with the all-purpose flour. Place the dough on the floured surface, and knead until the dough is smooth and forms a cohesive ball, about 30 seconds. Cut the dough into 16 equal pieces. Gently roll each piece into a smooth ball.

CONTINUED ▶

## Glazed Cinnamon Biscuit Bites continued

**4.** When the unit beeps to signify it has preheated, coat the basket well with cooking spray. Place 8 biscuit bites in the basket, leaving room between each, and spray each with cooking spray. Close the hood and cook for 10 to 12 minutes, until golden brown.

**5.** Meanwhile, in a medium mixing bowl, whisk together the powdered sugar and water until it forms a smooth glaze.

**6.** Gently remove the bites from the basket, and place them on a wire rack covered with aluminum foil. Repeat step 4 with the remaining biscuit bites.

**7.** Spoon half the glaze over the bites and let cool 5 minutes, then spoon over the remaining glaze.

*Per serving: Calories: 262; Total fat: 6g; Saturated fat: 4g; Cholesterol: 16mg; Sodium: 105mg; Carbohydrates: 50g; Fiber: 1g; Protein: 3g*

# Skillet Brownies

**SERVES 6 / PREP TIME:** 15 MINUTES / **TOTAL COOK TIME:** 40 MINUTES

*Whenever I'm asked for my favorite recipe to make in the original Ninja® Foodi™ Pressure Cooker, my answer is always the same—the Skillet Cookie. It may just be my favorite recipe ever: crisp and buttery on the outside, but ooey-gooey in the center. So when I started developing recipes for the Foodi Grill, I knew I had to create an equally delicious dessert. Enter the Skillet Brownie. With perfectly crisp, buttery edges and a fudgy middle, this recipe is a new favorite. Serve warm with a scoop of ice cream, or eat it right out of the pan with a big spoon.*

**NUT-FREE, VEGETARIAN, FAMILY FAVORITE**

**ACCESSORIES:** Ninja® Multi-Purpose Pan or 8-inch baking pan

- ½ cup all-purpose flour
- ¼ cup unsweetened cocoa powder
- ¾ teaspoon sea salt
- 2 large eggs
- 1 tablespoon water
- ½ cup granulated sugar
- ½ cup dark brown sugar
- 1 tablespoon vanilla extract
- 8 ounces semisweet chocolate chips, melted
- ¾ cup unsalted butter, melted
- Nonstick cooking spray

1. In a medium bowl, whisk together the flour, cocoa powder, and salt.

2. In a large bowl, whisk together the eggs, water, sugar, brown sugar, and vanilla until smooth.

3. In a microwave-safe bowl, melt the chocolate in the microwave. In a separate microwave-safe bowl, melt the butter.

4. In a separate medium bowl, stir together the chocolate and butter until evenly combined. Whisk into the egg mixture. Then slowly add the dry ingredients, stirring just until incorporated.

CONTINUED ▶

5. Remove the Grill Grate from the unit. Select BAKE, set the temperature to 350°F, and set the time to 40 minutes. Select START/STOP to begin preheating.

6. Meanwhile, lightly grease the Multi-Purpose Pan with cooking spray. Pour the batter into the pan, spreading evenly.

7. When the unit beeps to signify it has preheated, place the pan directly in the pot. Close the hood and cook for 40 minutes.

8. After 40 minutes, check that cooking is complete. A wooden toothpick inserted into the center of the brownies should come out clean.

Per serving: *Calories: 566; Total fat: 37g; Saturated fat: 22g; Cholesterol: 116mg; Sodium: 427mg; Carbohydrates: 63g; Fiber: 4g; Protein: 6g*

# Corn Bread Biscuits

**SERVES 6 / PREP TIME:** 15 MINUTES / **TOTAL COOK TIME:** 15 MINUTES

*These biscuits perfectly complement any of the grilled recipes in this book. Soft and flaky, they are best served warm and slathered with butter. Experiment by adding herbs, like sage, chives, or rosemary, to the batter.*

**NUT-FREE, VEGETARIAN, UNDER 30 MINUTES**

**ACCESSORIES:** Crisper Basket

**HACK IT:** Forgot to pick up buttermilk? Add 2 teaspoons of lemon juice to ⅔ cup of milk for a homemade substitute. Let it rest for a few minutes before using.

1½ cups all-purpose flour, plus additional for dusting

½ cup yellow cornmeal

2½ teaspoons baking powder

½ teaspoon sea salt

⅓ cup vegetable shortening

⅔ cup buttermilk

Nonstick cooking spray

1. In a large bowl, combine the flour, cornmeal, baking powder, and salt.

2. Add the shortening, and cut it into the flour mixture, until well combined and the dough resembles a coarse meal. Add the buttermilk and stir together just until moistened.

3. Insert the Crisper Basket and close the hood. Select AIR CRISP, set the temperature to 350ºF, and set the time to 15 minutes. Select START/STOP to begin preheating.

4. While the unit is preheating, dust a clean work surface with flour. Knead the mixture on the floured surface until a cohesive dough forms. Roll out the dough to an even thickness, then cut into biscuits with a 2-inch biscuit cutter.

5. When the unit beeps to signify it has preheated, coat the basket with cooking spray. Place 6 to 8 biscuits in the basket, well spaced, and spray each with cooking spray. Close the hood and cook for 12 to 15 minutes, until golden brown.

6. Gently remove the biscuits from the basket, and place them on a wire rack to cool. Repeat with the remaining dough.

*Per serving: Calories: 265; Total fat: 12g; Saturated fat: 4g; Cholesterol: 1mg; Sodium: 191mg; Carbohydrates: 34g; Fiber: 2g; Protein: 5g*

# Ninja® Foodi™ Grill
# MEAL PLAN AND SHOPPING LIST

To take full advantage of your Ninja Foodi Grill, use it to cook every meal! You can also download this meal plan and shopping list from www.callistomediabooks.com/NinjaFoodiGrill.

## MEAL PLAN

### Sunday

**Breakfast:** Grilled Pizza with Eggs and Greens 33
**Lunch:** Summer Vegetable Salad 73
**Dinner:** Grilled Swordfish in Caper Sauce and Blistered Green Beans 98 and 49
**Dessert:** Charred Peaches with Bourbon Butter Sauce 164

### Monday

**Breakfast:** Sausage and Egg Loaded Breakfast Pockets 36
**Lunch:** Lemon-Garlic Shrimp Caesar Salad 88
**Snack:** Fried Pickles 44
**Dinner:** Charred Korean-Style Steak Tips and Grilled Asian-Style Broccoli 155 and 52

### Tuesday

**Breakfast:** Grilled Fruit Salad with Honey-Lime Glaze 28
**Lunch:** Greek Chicken and Veggie Kebabs 112
**Dinner:** Cheesy Ranch Cauliflower Steaks 66
**Dessert:** Blueberry Cobbler 171

### Wednesday

**Breakfast:** Onion, Pepper, and Mushroom Frittata 29
**Lunch:** Grilled Broccoli and Arugula Salad 72
**Snack:** Sweet Potato Chips 61
**Dinner:** Honey-Glazed Pork Tenderloin and Bacon Brussels Sprouts 154 and 51

### Thursday

**Breakfast:** Baked Egg and Bacon–Stuffed Peppers 31

**Lunch:** Jalapeño Popper Burgers and Crispy Hand-Cut French Fries 156 and 59

**Dinner:** Honey-Lime Salmon with Avocado and Mango Salsa 95

**Dessert:** Glazed Cinnamon Biscuit Bites 179

### Friday

**Breakfast:** Grilled Cinnamon Toast with Berries and Whipped Cream 38

**Lunch:** Southwest Stuffed Peppers 76

**Snack:** Lemon-Garlic Artichokes 48

**Dinner:** Spicy Shrimp Tacos 89

### Saturday

**Breakfast:** Sausage Mixed Grill 35

**Lunch:** Cheesy Broccoli Calzones 81

**Dinner:** Filet Mignon with Pineapple Salsa and Crispy Rosemary Potatoes 141 and 56

**Dessert:** Grilled Pound Cake with Fresh Mint and Berries 166

## SHOPPING LIST

### Canned and Bottled Goods

- Beer (1 bottle)
- Bourbon (¼ cup)
- Capers (2 tablespoons)
- Coconut milk, full-fat, 1 (15-ounce) can
- Coconut milk, lite (¾ cup)
- Dressing, Caesar
- Dressing, ranch
- Honey (1 cup)
- Maple syrup (½ cup)
- Mustard, Dijon (1 teaspoon)
- Oil, avocado (½ tablespoon)
- Oil, canola (2 cups)
- Oil, extra-virgin olive (1 cup)
- Oil, nonstick cooking spray
- Oil, sesame (3 tablespoons)
- Oil, vegetable (2 tablespoons)
- Pickles, dill (20 round slices)
- Pineapple chunks (9-ounce can)
- Red enchilada sauce (10-ounce can)
- Soy sauce (⅔ cup)
- Stock, vegetable (½ cup)
- Vinegar, balsamic (¼ cup)

## Dairy and Eggs

- Butter, salted (1 stick)
- Butter, unsalted (3 sticks)
- Cheese, Cheddar, shredded (4 cups)
- Cheese, Colby Jack, shredded (8-ounce bag)
- Cheese, mozzarella, shredded (2 cups)
- Cheese, Parmesan, grated (1¼ cups)
- Cheese, pepper Jack (4 slices)
- Cheese, ricotta (1 cup)
- Cream cheese (4 ounces)
- Eggs (18)
- Milk, whole (1 pint)
- Yogurt, plain Greek, 1 (8-ounce) container

## Meat, Poultry, and Fish

- Bacon (18 slices)
- Beef, ground (2 pounds)
- Beef tips (1½ pounds)
- Chicken breasts, boneless, skinless (1 pound)
- Filet mignon steaks (4)
- Pork tenderloin (1½ pounds)
- Salmon, skinless, 4 (8-ounce) fillets
- Sausage, breakfast, ground (8 ounces)
- Sausage, breakfast links (6)
- Sausage, Italian, hot or sweet (6)
- Shrimp, jumbo (2 pounds)
- Swordfish, 4 (8-ounce) steaks

## Pantry Items

- Baking powder (3⅛ teaspoons)
- Black pepper, freshly ground
- Cayenne pepper (about ½ teaspoon)
- Celery salt (¼ teaspoon)
- Chili powder (1½ teaspoons)
- Cinnamon, ground (1 teaspoon)
- Coriander, ground
- Cornstarch (2 tablespoons)
- Cumin, ground (1 teaspoon)
- Flour, all-purpose (2½ cups)
- Flour, whole-wheat (⅔ cup)
- Garlic powder (2½ teaspoons)
- Onion powder (½ teaspoon)
- Oregano, dried (2 tablespoons)
- Paprika (1¾ teaspoons)
- Parsley, dried (½ teaspoon)
- Red pepper flakes
- Rosemary, dried (1 teaspoon)
- Sea salt
- Sesame seeds
- Southwestern seasoning (1 teaspoon)
- Sugar, brown (¾ cup)
- Sugar, granulated (1½ cups)
- Sugar, powdered (2⅛ cups)
- Vanilla extract (1½ teaspoons)

## Produce

- Apple (1)
- Artichokes (2 large)
- Arugula (8 cups)
- Avocado (2)
- Bell pepper (5)
- Bell pepper, mini (8)
- Bell pepper, red (7)
- Blueberries (5 cups)
- Broccoli (5 heads)
- Brussels sprouts (1 pound)
- Cabbage, green (2 cups shredded)
- Cauliflower (1 head)
- Chives (1 bunch)
- Cilantro (1 bunch)
- Corn (2 ears)
- Garlic (3 heads)
- Green beans (1 pound)
- Jalapeño peppers (4)
- Lemons (10)
- Limes (4)
- Mango (1)
- Mint, fresh (1 bunch)
- Mushrooms, cremini (4)
- Mushrooms, Portobello (2)
- Onion (2)
- Onion, red (4)
- Parsley (1 bunch)
- Peaches (6)
- Pineapple (1)
- Potatoes, red, baby (2 pounds)
- Potatoes, russet (1 pound)
- Potatoes, sweet (1)
- Radicchio (2 heads)
- Raspberries (1 cup)
- Romaine lettuce (2 heads)
- Scallions (1 bunch)
- Summer squash (1)
- Strawberries (1 pound)
- Tomato (1)
- Zucchini (2)

## Grains and Nuts

- Bread, challah (1 loaf)
- Bread crumbs, panko (1½ cups)
- Corn tortillas (4)
- Hamburger buns (4)
- Pecans, candied (¼ cup)
- Pound cake (6 slices)
- Rice, instant, 2 (8.5-ounce) bags
- Soft rolls (4)
- Sub rolls (4)

## Refrigerated

- Pizza dough (2½ pounds)

# Ninja® Foodi™ Grill
## COOKING CHARTS

## Grilling Chart

| INGREDIENT | AMOUNT | TEMP | COOK TIME | INSTRUCTIONS |
|---|---|---|---|---|
| **POULTRY**<br>Chart times are intended to cook poultry all the way through to an internal temperature of 165°F | | | | |
| Chicken breasts | 2 bone-in breasts (12–24 oz each) | HIGH | 16–20 mins | Flip halfway through cooking |
| | 4 boneless breasts (7–9 oz each) | HIGH | 14–18 mins | Flip halfway through cooking |
| Chicken, leg quarters | 2 bone-in leg quarters (12–14 oz each) | HIGH | 20–24 mins | Flip halfway through cooking |
| Chicken sausages, prepared | 1 package, 12 oz (4 sausages) | HIGH | 5–6 mins | Flipping not necessary |
| Chicken tenderloins | 6 boneless tenderloins (2–3 oz each) | HIGH | 7–10 mins | Flip halfway through cooking |
| Chicken thighs | 4 bone-in thighs (7–9 oz each) | HIGH | 23–26 mins | Flip halfway through cooking |
| | 4 boneless thighs (4–7 oz each) | HIGH | 10–13 mins | Flip halfway through cooking |
| Chicken wings | 2 lbs, bone-in (drumettes & flats) | HIGH | 10–14 mins | Flip halfway through cooking |
| Turkey burgers | 4 patties (¼ lb each), 1-inch thick | HIGH | 11–13 mins | Flipping not necessary |
| **BEEF**<br>Chart times are intended for to cook beef to medium doneness with an internal temperature of 145°F | | | | |
| Burgers | 4 patties (up to 7 oz each), 1–1½ inches thick | HIGH | 4–9 mins | Flipping not necessary |

| INGREDIENT | AMOUNT | TEMP | COOK TIME | INSTRUCTIONS |
|---|---|---|---|---|
| Filet mignon | 4 steaks (6-8 oz each); 1¼-1½ inches thick | HIGH | 12-15 mins | Flip halfway through cooking |
| Flat iron or flank steak | 2 steaks (8-10 oz each); 1-1¼ inches thick | HIGH | 7-10 mins | Flip halfway through cooking |
| Hot dogs | 4 hot dogs | HIGH | 3-5 mins | Flip halfway through cooking |
| NY strip | 2 steaks (14-16 oz each); 1¼-1½ inches thick | HIGH | 9-11 mins | Flip halfway through cooking |
| Rib eye | 2 steaks (14-16 oz each); 1¼ inches thick | HIGH | 8-10 mins | Flip halfway through cooking |
| Skirt | 2 steaks (8 oz each); ¾-1 inch thick | HIGH | 7-9 mins | Flip halfway through cooking |
| Steak tips | Up to 24 oz | MEDIUM | 11-13 mins | Marinate as desired |
| T-bone | 2 steaks (14-16 oz each); 1½ inches thick | HIGH | 9-12 mins | Flip halfway through cooking |
| **PORK, LAMB & VEAL** | | | | |
| Baby back ribs | 4 each, 3-bone pieces (8-10 oz) | HIGH | 20-22 mins | Flip halfway through cooking |
| Bacon | 5 strips; thick cut | LOW | 9-11 mins | Flipping not necessary |
| Lamb rack | ½ rack (4 bones) | HIGH | 12-14 mins | Flip halfway through cooking |
| Pork chops | 2 thick-cut, bone-in chops (10-12 oz each) | HIGH | 15-18 mins | Flip halfway through cooking |
| | 4 boneless chops (8 oz each) | HIGH | 14-16 mins | Flip halfway through cooking |
| Pork tenderloins | 2 whole tenderloins (1-1½ lbs each) | HIGH | 15-20 mins | Flip halfway through cooking |

| INGREDIENT | AMOUNT | TEMP | COOK TIME | INSTRUCTIONS |
|---|---|---|---|---|
| Sausages | 6 whole sausages (3–4 oz each) | LOW | 8–12 mins | Flip halfway through cooking |
| Veal chops | 4 bone-in chops (4–6 oz each) | HIGH | 8–12 mins | Flip halfway through cooking |
| **SEAFOOD** Chart times are intended to cook seafood all the way through to an internal temperature of 145°F | | | | |
| Cod or haddock | 4 fillets (4–6 oz each) | MAX | 8–10 mins | Flipping not necessary |
| Flounder | 2 fillets (2–4 oz each) | MAX | 2–3 mins | Flipping not necessary |
| Halibut | 4 fillets (4–6 oz each) | MAX | 6–9 mins | Flipping not necessary |
| Oysters | 12 | MAX | 5–7 mins | Shuck and place on grill, shell-side down |
| Salmon | 4 fillets (5–6 oz each) | MAX | 7–9 mins | Flipping not necessary |
| Scallops | 12 (1 lb) | MAX | 5–8 mins | Flip halfway through cooking |
| Shrimp | 1 lb jumbo (16–18 count) | MAX | 3–5 mins | Pat dry, season |
| Swordfish or tuna | 4 fillets (4–6 oz each) | MAX | 6–8 mins | Flipping not necessary |
| **FROZEN POULTRY** Chart times are intended to cook poultry all the way through to an internal temperature of 165°F | | | | |
| Chicken breasts | 4 boneless breasts (7–9 oz each) | MEDIUM | 20–25 mins | Flip 2 to 3 times while cooking |
| Chicken thighs | 4 bone-in thighs (7–9 oz each) | MEDIUM | 25–28 mins | Flip 2 to 3 times while cooking |
| Turkey burgers | 4 patties (4–6 oz each) | MEDIUM | 11–13 mins | Flip halfway through cooking, if desired |

| INGREDIENT | AMOUNT | TEMP | COOK TIME | INSTRUCTIONS |
|---|---|---|---|---|
| **FROZEN BEEF**<br>Chart times are intended to cook beef all the way through to an internal temperature of 145°F | | | | |
| **Burgers** | 4 patties (¼ lb each), 1 inch thick | MEDIUM | 10–15 mins | Flip halfway through cooking, if desired |
| **Filet mignon** | 2 steaks (6–8 oz each), 1¼–1½ inches thick | MEDIUM | 15–17 mins | Flip 2 to 3 times while cooking |
| **NY strip** | 2 steaks (14–16 oz each), 1¼–1½ inches thick | MEDIUM | 18–24 mins | Flip 2 to 3 times while cooking |
| **Rib eye** | 2 steaks (14–16 oz each), 1¼ inches thick | MEDIUM | 18–22 mins | Flip 2 to 3 times while cooking |
| **FROZEN PORK**<br>Chart times are intended to cook pork all the way through to an internal temperature of 145°F | | | | |
| **Pork chops** | 4 boneless chops (8 oz each) | MEDIUM | 20–23 mins | Flip 2 to 3 times while cooking |
| **Pork tenderloin** | 1 whole tenderloin (1 lb) | MEDIUM | 20 mins | Flip 2 to 3 times while cooking |
| **Sausage, uncooked** | 6 whole sausages (approx. 1 lb) | LOW | 10–14 mins | Flip halfway through cooking |
| **FROZEN SEAFOOD**<br>Chart times are intended to cook seafood all the way through to an internal temperature of 145°F | | | | |
| **Halibut** | 4 fillets (6 oz each) | MAX | 14–16 mins | Flip halfway through cooking, if desired |
| **Salmon** | 4 fillets (4 oz each) | MAX | 10–13 mins | Flip halfway through cooking, if desired |
| **Shrimp** | 1 lb jumbo (16–18 each) | MAX | 4–6 mins | Flipping not necessary |
| **FROZEN VEGGIE BURGERS** | | | | |
| **Veggie burgers** | 4 patties (4 oz each) | HIGH | 8–10 mins | Flip halfway through cooking, if desired |

| INGREDIENT | AMOUNT | PREPARATION | TEMP | COOK TIME | INSTRUCTIONS |
|---|---|---|---|---|---|
| VEGETABLES | | | | | |
| Asparagus | 1 bunch | Whole, trim stems | MAX | 5–7 mins | Flipping not necessary |
| Baby bok choy | 1 lb | Cut in half lengthwise, season | MAX | 9–11 mins | Flip halfway through cooking |
| Bell peppers | 3 | Cut in quarters, season | MAX | 10–12 mins | Flip halfway through cooking |
| Broccoli | 2 heads (1 lb) | Cut in 2-inch florets | MAX | 10 mins | Flipping not necessary |
| Brussels sprouts | 2 lbs | Whole, trim stems | MAX | 12–15 mins | Flip halfway through cooking |
| Carrots | 6 (1½ lb) | Peel, cut in 2–3-inch pieces, season | MAX | 12 mins | Flipping not necessary |
| Cauliflower | 1 head (12–16 oz) | Cut in 2-inch florets | MAX | 12–15 mins | Flipping not necessary |
| Corn on the cob | 4–5 | Whole ears, remove husks | MAX | 10–13 mins | Flip halfway through cooking |
| Crimini mushrooms | 1 lb | Cut in half, season | MAX | 5–7 mins | Flipping not necessary |
| Eggplant | 1 large (12–16 oz) | Cut in 2-inch pieces, season | MAX | 10–12 mins | Flip halfway through cooking |
| Green Beans | 24 oz | Trim stems, season | MAX | 8–10 mins | Flipping not necessary |
| Onions, white or red (cut in half) | 5 | Peel, cut in half, season | MAX | 10–12 mins | Flipping not necessary |

| INGREDIENT | AMOUNT | PREPARATION | TEMP | COOK TIME | INSTRUCTIONS |
|---|---|---|---|---|---|
| Onions, white or red (sliced) | 1-2 | Peel, cut in 1-inch slices, season | MAX | 2-4 mins | Flip halfway through cooking |
| Portobella mushrooms | 4 | Remove stems, scrape out gills with spoon, season | MAX | 8 mins | Flip halfway through cooking |
| Squash or Zucchini | 4-5 (24 oz) | Cut in quarters lengthwise, season | MAX | 12-16 mins | Flip halfway through cooking |
| Tomatoes | 5 | Cut in half, season | MAX | 8-10 mins | Flipping not necessary |
| **FRUIT** | | | | | |
| Avocado | Up to 3 avocados | Cut in half, remove pit | HIGH | 4-5 mins | Flipping not necessary |
| Bananas | 4 | Peel, cut in half lengthwise | MAX | 2 mins | Remove using silicone-tipped tongs or spatula |
| Lemons & Limes | 5 | Cut in half lengthwise, press down on Grill Grate | MAX | 3 mins | Flipping not necessary |
| Mango | 4-6 | Press down gently on Grill Grate | MAX | 4 mins | Flipping not necessary |
| Melon | 6 spears (4-6 inches each) | Press down gently on Grill Grate | MAX | 4 mins | Flipping not necessary |
| Pineapple | 6-8 slices or spears | Cut in 2-inch pieces | MAX | 7-9 mins | Flip gently several times during cooking |
| Stone fruit (such as peaches & plums) | 4-6 | Cut in half, remove pit, press down on Grill Grate | MAX | 10-12 mins | Flipping not necessary |

| INGREDIENT | AMOUNT | PREPARATION | TEMP | COOK TIME | INSTRUCTIONS |
|---|---|---|---|---|---|
| **BREAD & CHEESE** | | | | | |
| Bread | 2–3 slices | Hand-cut, 2-inch slices, brushed with canola oil | MAX | 3–4 mins | Flipping not necessary |
| Halloumi cheese | 1 lb | Cut in 1-inch slices | HIGH | 4 mins | Flipping not necessary |

## Air Crisping Chart

| INGREDIENT | AMOUNT | PREPARATION | TOSS IN OIL | TEMP | COOK TIME |
|---|---|---|---|---|---|
| **VEGETABLES** | | | | | |
| Asparagus | 2 bunches | Whole, trim stems | 2 tsp | 390°F | 12–14 mins |
| Beets | 6 small or 4 large (about 2 lbs) | Whole | None | 390°F | 45–60 mins |
| Bell peppers | 4 | Whole | None | 400°F | 20–25 mins |
| Broccoli | 2 heads | Cut in 1-inch florets | 1 tbsp | 390°F | 12–16 mins |
| Brussels sprouts | 2 lbs | Cut in half, remove stems | 1 tbsp | 390°F | 15–18 mins |
| Butternut squash | 3 lbs | Cut in 1–2-inch pieces | 1 tbsp | 390°F | 30 mins |
| Carrots | 2 lbs | Peel, cut in ½-inch pieces | 1 tbsp | 390°F | 16–18 mins |
| Cauliflower | 2 heads | Cut in 1-inch florets | 2 tbsp | 390°F | 20–24 mins |
| Corn on the cob | 5 | Whole ears, remove husks | 1 tbsp | 390°F | 12–15 mins |

| INGREDIENT | AMOUNT | PREPARATION | TOSS IN OIL | TEMP | COOK TIME |
|---|---|---|---|---|---|
| Green beans | 2 bags (24 oz) | Trim | 1 tbsp | 390°F | 10–12 mins |
| Kale (for chips) | 8 cups, packed | Tear in pieces, remove stems | None | 300°F | 10–12 mins |
| Mushrooms | 1 lb | Rinse, cut in quarters | 1 tbsp | 390°F | 10–12 mins |
| Potatoes, russet | 3 lbs | Cut in 1-inch wedges | 1 tbsp | 390°F | 25–30 mins |
| | 1 lb | Hand-cut fries, thin | ½–3 tbsp, canola | 390°F | 20–24 mins |
| | 1 lb | Hand-cut fries, thick | ½–3 tbsp, canola | 390°F | 23–26 mins |
| | 4 whole (6–8 oz) | Pierce with fork 3 times | None | 390°F | 38–42 mins |
| Potatoes, sweet | 1½ lbs | Cut in 1-inch chunks | 1 tbsp | 390°F | 15–20 mins |
| | 6 whole (6-8 oz) | Pierce with fork 3 times | None | 390°F | 30–35 mins |
| Zucchini | 2 lbs | Cut in quarters lengthwise, then cut in 1-inch pieces | 1 tbsp | 390°F | 15–18 mins |
| POULTRY | | | | | |
| Chicken breasts | 2 breasts (¾–1½ lbs each) | Bone in | Brushed with oil | 375°F | 25–35 mins |
| | 2 breasts (½–¾ lb each) | Boneless | Brushed with oil | 375°F | 18–22 mins |
| Chicken thighs | 4 thighs (6–10 oz each) | Bone in | Brushed with oil | 390°F | 22–28 mins |
| | 4 thighs (4–8 oz each) | Boneless | Brushed with oil | 390°F | 18–22 mins |
| Chicken wings | 2 lbs (drumettes & flats) | Bone in | 1 tbsp | 390°F | 22–26 mins |

| INGREDIENT | AMOUNT | PREPARATION | TOSS IN OIL | TEMP | COOK TIME |
|---|---|---|---|---|---|
| **PORK & LAMB** | | | | | |
| Bacon | 4 strips, cut in half | None | None | 350°F | 8–10 mins |
| Pork chops | 2 thick-cut, bone-in chops (10–12 oz each) | Bone in | Brush with oil | 375°F | 15–17 mins |
| | 4 boneless chops (8 oz each) | Boneless | Brush with oil | 375°F | 14–17 mins |
| Pork tenderloins | 2 tenderloins (1–1½ lbs each) | Whole | Brush with oil | 375°F | 25–35 mins |
| Sausages | 4 sausages | Whole | None | 390°F | 8–10 mins |
| **FROZEN FOODS** | | | | | |
| Chicken cutlets | 5 cutlets | None | None | 390°F | 18–21 mins |
| Chicken nuggets | 1 box (12 oz) | None | None | 390°F | 10–13 mins |
| Fish fillets | 1 box (6 fillets) | None | None | 390°F | 14–16 mins |
| Fish sticks | 18 fish sticks (11 oz; approx. 1 box) | None | None | 390°F | 10–13 mins |
| French fries | 1 lb | None | None | 350°F | 20–25 mins |
| | 2 lbs | None | None | 360°F | 28–32 mins |
| Mozzarella sticks | 1 box (11 oz) | None | None | 375°F | 8–10 mins |
| Pot stickers | 1 bag (24 oz, 20 count) | None | None | 390°F | 12–14 mins |
| Pizza rolls | 1 bag (20 oz, 40 count) | None | None | 390°F | 12–15 mins |
| Popcorn shrimp | 1 box (14–16 oz) | None | None | 390°F | 9–11 mins |

| INGREDIENT | AMOUNT | PREPARATION | TOSS IN OIL | TEMP | COOK TIME |
|---|---|---|---|---|---|
| Sweet potato fries | 1 lb | None | None | 375°F | 20–22 mins |
| Tater tots | 1 lb | None | None | 360°F | 18–22 mins |

## Dehydrating Chart

| INGREDIENTS | PREPARATION | TEMP | DEHYDRATE TIME |
|---|---|---|---|
| **FRUITS & VEGETABLES** | | | |
| Apples | Cut in ⅛-inch slices, remove core, rinse in lemon water, pat dry | 135°F | 7–8 hours |
| Asparagus | Cut in 1-inch pieces, blanch | 135°F | 6–8 hours |
| Bananas | Peel, cut in ⅜-inch slices | 135°F | 8–10 hours |
| Beets | Peel, cut in ⅛-inch slices | 135°F | 6–8 hours |
| Eggplant | Peel, cut in ¼-inch slices, blanch | 135°F | 6–8 hours |
| Fresh herbs | Rinse, pat dry, remove stems | 135°F | 4 hours |
| Ginger root | Cut in ⅜-inch slices | 135°F | 6 hours |
| Mangoes | Peel, cut in ⅜-inch slices, remove pit | 135°F | 6–8 hours |
| Mushrooms | Clean with soft brush (do not wash) | 135°F | 6–8 hours |
| Pineapple | Peel, cut in slices, remove core | 135°F | 6–8 hours |
| Strawberries | Cut in half or in ½-inch slices | 135°F | 6–8 hours |
| Tomatoes | Cut in ⅜-inch slices or grated; steam if planning to rehydrate | 135°F | 6–8 hours |

| INGREDIENTS | PREPARATION | TEMP | DEHYDRATE TIME |
|---|---|---|---|
| **MEAT, POULTRY, FISH** | | | |
| Beef jerky | Cut in ¼-inch slices, marinate overnight | 150°F | 5–7 hours |
| Chicken jerky | Cut in ¼-inch slices, marinate overnight | 150°F | 5–7 hours |
| Turkey jerky | Cut in ¼-inch slices, marinate overnight | 150°F | 5–7 hours |
| Salmon jerky | Cut in ¼-inch slices, marinate overnight | 150°F | 3–5 hours |

# MEASUREMENT CONVERSIONS

## VOLUME EQUIVALENTS (LIQUID)

| US Standard | US Standard (ounces) | Metric (approximate) |
|---|---|---|
| 2 tablespoons | 1 fl. oz. | 30 mL |
| ¼ cup | 2 fl. oz. | 60 mL |
| ½ cup | 4 fl. oz. | 120 mL |
| 1 cup | 8 fl. oz. | 240 mL |
| 1½ cups | 12 fl. oz. | 355 mL |
| 2 cups or 1 pint | 16 fl. oz. | 475 mL |
| 4 cups or 1 quart | 32 fl. oz. | 1 L |
| 1 gallon | 128 fl. oz. | 4 L |

## OVEN TEMPERATURES

| Fahrenheit (F) | Celsius (C) (approximate) |
|---|---|
| 250°F | 120°C |
| 300°F | 150°C |
| 325°F | 165°C |
| 350°F | 180°C |
| 375°F | 190°C |
| 400°F | 200°C |
| 425°F | 220°C |
| 450°F | 230°C |

## VOLUME EQUIVALENTS (DRY)

| US Standard | Metric (approximate) |
|---|---|
| ⅛ teaspoon | 0.5 mL |
| ¼ teaspoon | 1 mL |
| ½ teaspoon | 2 mL |
| ¾ teaspoon | 4 mL |
| 1 teaspoon | 5 mL |
| 1 tablespoon | 15 mL |
| ¼ cup | 59 mL |
| ⅓ cup | 79 mL |
| ½ cup | 118 mL |
| ⅔ cup | 156 mL |
| ¾ cup | 177 mL |
| 1 cup | 235 mL |
| 2 cups or 1 pint | 475 mL |
| 3 cups | 700 mL |
| 4 cups or 1 quart | 1 L |

## WEIGHT EQUIVALENTS

| US Standard | Metric (approximate) |
|---|---|
| ½ ounce | 15 g |
| 1 ounce | 30 g |
| 2 ounces | 60 g |
| 4 ounces | 115 g |
| 8 ounces | 225 g |
| 12 ounces | 340 g |
| 16 ounces or 1 pound | 455 g |

# INDEX

# ACKNOWLEDGMENTS

First and foremost, thank you to Julien, my best friend, my faithful taste tester, my cameraman, and my husband. Thank you for supporting me through late nights of copywriting and long days of recipe testing.

To my friends and family, thank you for your words of encouragement and for cheering for me throughout this journey. I am so thankful to have each and every one of you in my corner.

To my amazing team at Ninja®—Sam, Corey, Meg, Craig, Chelven, and Caroline—thank you for inspiring me every day. Thank you for supporting my wild ideas, for making me excited to come to work, and for filling the world with flavorful recipes.

To Bridget and my team at Callisto Media, thank you for joining me on this journey and for believing in this product. I am so happy to be working with you again and am proud to be part of the Callisto Media family.

Last but never least, to my readers, thank you for trying my recipes and sharing them with your friends and loved ones. I hope you love the Ninja® Foodi™ Grill and these recipes as much as I do!

# ABOUT THE AUTHOR

 **KENZIE SWANHART** is a home cook turned food blogger and cookbook author providing her readers with inspiration in and out of the kitchen. With more than 250,000 copies of her cookbooks in print, Kenzie never wavers in her mission: creating and sharing easy yet flavorful recipes made with real ingredients with her readers.

As the head of culinary marketing and innovation for Ninja, a leading kitchen appliance company, Kenzie and her team provide a unique, food-first point of view for the development of new products and recipes to make consumers' lives easier and healthier. You'll also see her serving as the face of Ninja on the leading television home shopping network, where she shares tips, tricks, and recipes for the company's full line of products.

Kenzie lives in Boston with her husband, Julien, and their dog, Charlie.